Marriage Glue

By Tania Chapman Scott

Endorsements

Marriage Glue is a must read. It doesn't matter if you're newlyweds, been married 60 years, or if you're single and desire to become married someday, you can learn something from this book to keep your marriage (or future marriage) on track.

Having been married over 35 years, we can attest to strategies for healthy marriages discussed in this phenomenally amazing book. Tania transparently lays it all on the line and shares personal and relatable marriage experiences. This book is a true testament of the redemptive power of God to heal marriages and bring fulfillment through Christ.

Marriage Glue will point you to the word of God with references and practical applications for successful marriages.

No other book we've read on marriage provides such clear, genuine, and proven strategies the way *Marriage Glue* does.

As you read this book, we pray the Holy Spirit will enlighten your hearts with His plan and purpose for your lives and marriages.

Pastor Art and Amanda Dyson
Ephesians Christian Center, Los Angeles, CA
www.Ephesianscc.com

In *Marriage Glue*, Tania Scott provides relevant instruction and encouragement for every married person who desires to grow. Her use of scriptures, personal experiences, and a "little flare" invites the reader to not only engage while reading, but to also apply when done so you can stick to God and your spouse.

Kenneth Mulkey,
Pastor, Author, Coach
Cottonwood Church, Los Alamitos, CA

Contents

Acknowledgments

Thanks to all of my family, friends, and the prayer warriors on the Thursday Night prayer line, for their prayers and support while I was writing this book.

I also want to thank Pastor Art and First Lady Amanda Dyson of Ephesians Christian Church of Los Angeles, California for being so supportive during this process, and for allowing me to speak about *Marriage Glue* with their church.

And thank you, Pastor Kenneth Mulkey of my church, Cottonwood Church of Los Alamitos, California for giving his support as our assistant pastor and as a fellow author.

I am eternally grateful for my husband, Gordon Scott, and for our adult children, Allison, Blake, and Celeste for enduring the transition with me as a new author. Whose technical, administrative, emotional, and spiritual support were key to my completing this work.

Lastly, thank you to my agent and editor, Dr. Sharon Norris Elliott of AuthorizeMe Literary Firm of Los Angeles, California, for the care and effort put into editing this, my debut book.

Dedication

This book is dedicated to my Heavenly Father, Who showed me that I could have a happy, godly marriage despite not seeing one as a child. To my husband, Gordon, for constantly reminding me that God called me to write this book, so I had better finish it. To my A-B-C kids, Allison, Blake, and Celeste for being the wind beneath my wings. And finally, I dedicate this book to my parents. My mom, Erma Jean, for teaching me diligence and how to be a woman of prayer. And to my dad, Grady Chapman, for giving me the creative gene, and for giving me some very good advice.

A Note of Caution

Nothing is impossible with God. Know that as a fact. Also know that we are living in a world that has been affected by the sickness of sin, and sickness, unfortunately, flows into every area of our lives if we let it. If you have been a victim of physical abuse, substance abuse by your spouse, or the constant threat of physical violence (implied or expressed) upon your person or your children or other family members, I want to warn you that this book is not suggesting you physically stay in harm's way. I do not want to be misunderstood.

I am not a proponent of staying in a marriage under any and all circumstances. No! For extreme cases such as those outlined above, you need to seek professional Christian counseling and seek direct guidance from the Holy Spirit and God Himself, through prayer, as to how you should proceed in your marriage. I believe certain situations and marriages are outside of God's will because perhaps you were not seeking God's counsel and blessing when you initially got into them. This does not mean God isn't big enough to turn these extreme situations around for some couples, for God's word says, "There is nothing too hard for You [God]" (Jeremiah 32:17). "If you can believe, all things are possible to him who believes" (Mark 9:23).

In other words, this book was not written for serious problems that can occur within some marriages, such as physical abuse or even adultery, because that has not been my personal experience. I do not want to be the author who writes about things and situations that he or she has not experienced, at least to some extent and then pretends to be an expert in that area.

That said, I do believe many marriages have been ended for reasons other than the serious ones stated above. My marriage almost ended, and it wasn't because of infidelity or some other serious reason. According to a journal article published in *Couple and Family Practice: Research and Practice*, when 52 divorced individuals were interviewed, who had participated in a relationship education program while engaged, it was determined that the most common reasons cited for divorce were "lack of commitment, infidelity, and conflict/arguing." While the sample consisted of 52 people, it showed a noticeable pattern. Some marriages are ending when they did not have to. Lack of commitment, conflict/arguing, unmet needs, feeling like you're incompatible, to name a few, are all types of problems covered in this book. I want to approach your marriage (and mine too) from the standpoint of, "What does the Word of God say about your marriage?" Too often, we decide to just take our marital issues and problems into our own hands, but are we considering what God wants?

Let's imagine you purchased a well-crafted and expensive automobile—and deciding to ignore the operation manual— you just drove the car while never getting it serviced. I am sure you can imagine the manufacturer, or even your friends and family, trying to understand why or how you found it necessary to ruin this precious creation of a car. In this illustration, the manufacturer represents God, and His precious creation is marriage. In fact, I believe God looks at your marriage as being His own 'merch' as the young people say. You and your spouse are representing Him if to no one else but your children and family members. But most likely to many others.

Married women, you must understand the importance of not taking lightly the serious nature of your wedding vows and the fact that God takes our promises to Him very seriously. We must give our very best effort to bring God into our situation. But we must also work on ourselves in the process, asking God to help us to change, and find our own individual purpose, in the process. We will explore God's original plan for marriage, in Chapter 3, when we ask the question, "God, Is *This* What You Had in Mind?" What God says about divorce is also covered later, in Chapter 9.

I've written this book to let you know that if you simply give up on your marriage, God will not be pleased with your decision. It could represent one of the biggest failures you will ever experience in your life. I honestly believe that God will ask you about it on Judgement Day. I know that sounds deep, but I believe that He will. And you will be allowing Satan the adversary to win the victory in your marriage if you're not careful. The Bible says in Galatians 6:9 "And let us not get tired of doing what is right, for after a while we will reap a harvest of blessing if we don't get discouraged and give up" (TLB). This is a promise placed in the Bible for us to believe and hold on to for our lives, and that includes our marriages.

There's also another promise we can hold on to, "But no weapon that is formed against you shall prosper, and every tongue that shall rise against you in judgment you shall show to be in the wrong. This [peace, righteousness, security, triumph over opposition] is the heritage of the servants of the Lord [those in whom the ideal Servant of the Lord is reproduced]; this is the righteousness or the vindication which they obtain from Me [this is that which I impart to them as their justification] says the Lord." (Isaiah 54:17 AMP) That means that no attack from the enemy against your marriage and your family will be able to stand against God's omnipotent power and protection, when you belong to Him and have done your best to do His will.

If you are still holding this book, I believe the Holy Spirit has led you to read it and will give you revelation and understanding along the way. I strongly believe that God Himself had me to write this book. Why? Read on, and I will tell you.

Chapter One

But Ma', You didn't Tell Me it Would be Like This!
Part 1 – The Pain and the Promise

I was tired — tired of praying and tired of waiting on God to work a miracle in my marriage. I had come to a place where I was seriously looking for an exit. I felt like I had given it a pretty darn good try at holding things together and yet, I had grown weary. I didn't actually want to leave, but I felt like staying any longer would only result in more wasted years. I wanted to be happy and happily married. As thoughts in this manner circled through my mind for several months, I would periodically run across this scripture in my Bible:

Lord, who may dwell in your sanctuary?

Who may live on your holy hill?

He whose walk is blameless and who does what is righteous

Who speaks the truth from his heart and has no slander on his tongue,

Who does his neighbor no wrong and casts no slur on his fellowman,

Who despises a vile man but honors those who fear the Lord,

Who keeps his oath (his promise) even when it hurts

He who does these things will never be shaken. (Psalm 15: 1 – 5, NIV)

Whenever I would read this passage, I knew God was speaking to me about my marriage vows—the *promises* I had made to my husband before God and all the witnesses present at our ceremony. God was saying to me, "The person who can dwell in my presence is the one who can keep his (or her) promises, even when it hurts to keep them." He goes on to say that a person who keeps his promises will never be moved or shaken. In this context, the Bible is speaking of a promise made to God, and it is the promises we make to Him that are the most important to Him. God was letting me know He cared that I kept the promises I made on that beautiful day in September of 1990, my wedding day. Unfortunately, now in my life, I could really relate to the part about it hurting to keep the promise.

Part 2 – Living on Fantasy Island

As a very young girl, I remember wanting to get married and have children when I grew up. I even had a Madam Alexander bride doll named Leslie, an African American doll with the prettiest brown face and sparkling brown eyes. She epitomized the beauty and elegance of a bride on her wedding day, wearing a mesh wedding gown, lace bodice and lace trim, complete with a lace-trimmed veil and a tiara made of silk flowers. Oh, and she even had a "diamond" solitaire wedding ring! The fact that I had this doll lets me know many other young girls must have had a bride doll like her as well.

When you think about it, as girls, we were playing with dolls and playing "house," while boys our age were playing with toy soldiers, getting dirty outside, playing with worms, or doing something else gross! At the root of many of the problems women face in marriage is the fact that as little girls, many of us watched too many fairy tales on television. We formed our marriage fantasies as little girls gazing at Leslie the bride doll, imagining how beautiful and wonderful we would be as brides. After we got engaged, we were still walking around with that perfect fantasy in our hearts. Focusing mainly on the wedding ceremony, our wedding dress, and the ring. But we didn't go beyond that end scene in Cinderella and Snow White (and many romance movies after we grew up), where the handsome young prince carried the beautiful princess off into the perfectly colored sunset to live happily ever after.

It's not so funny that those storylines never showed what happened to the couple after that ride into the sunset. Because we made those fairy tale fantasies our norm for reality, when we got married, we actually expected our prince charming to carry us off on his white horse (well maybe a white Rolls Royce or stretch limo), treat us like princesses, and we'd live happily ever after.

So, when the first argument with our new spouse came up, we were not prepared for this glitch in the plot. We began to put the blame on him. Surely, something was wrong with this prince. We began to think, *This one must not have been adequately programmed to what was written in my fantasy.* By now, we'd forgotten how the fantasy came to be ours in the first place, how it was acquired from reading fairy tales while we were small girls still in pigtails and playing with dolls, enriched by watching romcoms as we got older.

Barbie never had any problems with Ken.

One of the first disagreements I had with my husband Gordon was about taking out the trash. I asked Gordon to take out the trash and he replied that he was going to take it out, but when he got ready to do it, not when I thought it was time. Well, that just wasn't written into my fantasy. My fantasy had the husband taking out the trash daily and I never had to worry about that chore. After all, that was the man's job, right? Well, maybe five years or so into our marriage, I had to begin to accept the fact that trash duty was just not one of my husband's strong points and if I wanted the trash emptied daily, the best person for that job was me!

My point here is not to infer that our fantasies, or ideas of what we would like our marriages to be like, need be completely thrown out of the window. It's just to point out that many thoughts that we have about married life are simply that – fantasies – based on childish fairy tales and dreams. Unfortunately, reality does not measure up to fiction in any way shape or form. No matter how perfect your prince charming may appear to be.

I will say though, this is something I feel like only we women can relate to. It's very difficult to accept when you've carried around, as part of your inner psychic, this ideal situation of how you want to be treated as a bride – beyond the wedding day – and reality doesn't match up. No woman gets married thinking or wanting to accept something less than her fantasy of how she always thought married life would be. This is when many women might decide that it's time for "Plan B." It's time for another husband, or perhaps just someone different in their lives. Maybe even a lover or "special friend" of some sort. (In chapter six, I discuss more on this topic.) But, unfortunately – and I say unfortunately because it can be a very hard pill to swallow – God wants more from us than just taking the seemingly easy way out. Also, I would be remiss if I didn't tell you the Bible teaches us, "There is a way that seems right to a man (woman), but its end is the way of death." (Proverbs 14:12) Be careful that what you may begin to justify in your mind as being right, isn't what the Bible calls sin! So, let's begin to dive in a little bit deeper and analyze a few problems in our thinking that we may need to correct within ourselves first!

Unspoken, Unmet Expectations

When I got married, I thought marriage would be one long series of loveable moments. We would talk endlessly about our feelings, and our plans for the future. Gordon would carry my purse for me while I shopped happily and endlessly, like those husbands I would see in the department stores. We would always be together. And there would never be any secrets kept from each other (even though I had a few that I didn't share with him.) After all, this was the man that I had prayed for and surely God had found my perfect match. So of course, I didn't need to go over these unspoken expectations, right?

As engaged women, all we thought about was we had this wonderful guy who checked most (if not all) of our "boxes" of what we were looking for in a husband. But the boxes represented what we wanted outwardly in a husband. For example, we may have been looking for someone who is handsome, of a certain height, a professional career, someone who goes to church, of a certain complexion, or who has "pretty hair." My prayer for my husband consisted of only two main things: Number one, he needed to work! And number two, he had to go to church.

I had my reasons for my two most important criteria. And they had very much to do with my personal experiences growing up, and after becoming an adult. It was because I noticed way more women in church than men, and because of the fact that I wasn't raised in church. Additionally, I did not want to be married to someone and come home from work one day and he end up telling me, "I quit my job. I just think I need to find myself"! That just was not going to work for me. I had seen my very hard-working mother, have to raise me as a single parent. So, it was very important to me that my husband be responsible as well. Those two traits were like my only two "boxes" that I had to check off about my future husband, but there were others that were contained in my mind of what marriage should be – many others.

In chapter five, I am going to go into a lot more detail about common unrealistic expectations in marriage, and we are going to separate the biblical ones from ones that are just from the movies or somebody's social media page that we've been looking at. For now, can we agree that some of our problems just may be that we have been living on Fantasy Island? I know, I am one of the first who will admit that I have had this problem. Especially with a name that means "fairy princess"!

Part 3 – All I Need is a New Husband

It hurts when your marriage or your husband does not turn out to be exactly what you dreamed of for years. The frustration sometimes drives you to want to simply throw in the towel, or perhaps trade in your current prince charming for another more well-suited character. But who knows whether Prince #2 will be any better than Prince #1? Who knows if the new model will bring you total happiness? God knows, and often the answer is, "No, it will not."

I am reminded of the Samaritan woman who Jesus met at Jacob's well, while on His way to Galilee. Jesus had been tired from walking all morning, and at about noon, He saw this woman at the well. They had an interesting conversation that began with Him asking her for some water. She replied with a question: How could He be asking a Samaritan woman for anything? The Jews considered Samaritans like pagans, and Jews did not associate with them. Also, she was a woman who had come to the well alone, which would be a red flag that she was an outcast, and not accepted by the other women.

But here Jesus was having a conversation with her, which was not something any other Jewish priest would have done. And yet, here He was asking her to give Him some water! Jesus then told her that if she knew the gift God had for her and exactly who it was that was asking her for a drink, she would instead be asking *Him* for *living* water! The kind of water that causes you to never thirst again. The conversation goes on, but Jesus was hinting at something when he told her about His living water. He knew that she had been "thirsty" for some time. The rest of the conversation went on like this:

> "...Please, sir," the woman said, "give me this water! Then I'll never be thirsty again, and I won't have to come here to get water." "Go and get your husband," Jesus told her. "I don't have a husband," the woman replied. Jesus said, "You're right! You don't have a husband— for you have had five husbands, and you aren't even married to the man you're living with now. You certainly spoke the truth!" "Sir," the woman said, "you must be a prophet." (John 4: 15 – 19 NLT)

The woman then asked Jesus about the correct place to worship. But Jesus, who was known for cutting through the red tape of manmade religion, answered her:

> "... "Believe me, dear woman, the time is coming when it will no longer matter whether you worship the Father on this mountain or in Jerusalem... But the time is coming—indeed it's here now—when true worshipers will worship the Father in spirit and in truth. The Father is looking for those who will worship him that way. ... For God is Spirit, so those who worship him must worship in spirit and in truth." The woman said, "I know the Messiah is coming— the one who is called Christ. When he comes, he will explain everything to us." Then Jesus told

her, "I AM the Messiah!" The woman then left her water jar beside the well and ran back to the village, telling everyone, "Come and see a man who told me everything I ever did! Could he possibly be the Messiah?" So, the people came streaming from the village to see him." (John 4: 21, 23 – 26, 28 – 30 NLT)

Girlfriend! I truly pray that you will get this part! This woman had had *five* husbands and not *one* of them had been able to satisfy her thirst. Of course, I don't mean human thirst. But what I do mean is that she was looking for something that she would only find in one Man! When she had this encounter with the Messiah, He let her know that He had been aware of her problems, her struggles, and the shame of having been married and re-married all of those times. He knew that she needed Him to intervene in her situation and tell her the real thing that she was missing.

What she was missing was someone who knew all about her, but yet still took the time to talk with her, be patient with her, love and accept her unconditionally. She knew *about* the Messiah, but she needed to have a personal encounter with Him. The Savior who could not only do all these things that I mentioned, but He also could free her from all of the "water jars" that were weighing her down! She forgot why she had come to the well in the first place. She wasn't thirsty anymore! She was satiated. Filled with the goodness of God. And not only that, but she also ended up being the catalyst to hundreds (maybe even thousands) of people from her city believing in Jesus!

The primary goal of this book is to tell you this: All of your hopes and desires, the disappointments, and the failures within your marriage (or within your own life) – Jesus already knows about them! And your Savior alone is the one Who will be able to fix them. Your husband, as much as he is capable of loving you in his own way, cannot begin to *totally* fulfill you. But Jesus can! And all you have to do is have that one impactful encounter with Him that changes your life! But you have to make the time to be where you're supposed to be when you need to be there.

Well, you might say, this woman was just on her way to get water for drinking! And you'd be right! Yes, Jesus can meet you in the most unexpected places. But at the same time, she could've said I'm too embarrassed to keep going to the well by myself. The other women look at me and laugh and whisper when I go to the well at noon, instead of early in the morning like they do. She kept going to the well though, every day at noon. And she ended up meeting with her destiny! Where are you supposed to be? Maybe you're supposed to continue attending your church or continue praying for your marriage, or maybe you're supposed to continue reading this book! I believe that you are, because God called me to write it to help you and your marriage.

"At least 50% of the problems you are experiencing in your marriage are your fault.," a wise person once said. Have you ever heard the saying, "It takes two to tango"? Another wise saying I've heard is this, "No matter where you go, no matter how far you travel away, when you arrive, when you step off of that plane, guess who's always there to greet you? You!" You cannot get away from yourself! No matter how many times you change your partner or husband, you are still going to be a part of the union. Some of the same types of problems are going to surface and perhaps worse. We will look at the statistics of successful second (or third) marriages, in chapter nine. But now, let's look at something that we should have been taught, prior to our wedding day.

Part 4 – No One Taught Me How to be a Wife

Something that can cause problems within your marriage, is if you were not raised in a home where a father figure was present. Wives who were raised in a home with both parents, had a bigger chance of learning how to treat a man and how a woman is to be treated as well. So, if you weren't raised by your father or a father figure who set a good example, you probably had little practice learning how to be a wife and how to treat your husband. As was my experience.

My parents weren't married. My mom had been married for a short time before she met my dad, but it had not been a good marriage. So inevitably, my mother ended up making very generalized statements to me about how a man was supposed to treat me. And she failed to mention what *my* role should be.

Even if your parents were married, perhaps your mother was not able to sit down with you and share the things she learned throughout her marriage. But at least if you were raised by both parents, you would have had an example to follow. And hopefully it was a good one.

Additionally, in homes without a father figure, there is no division of duties. The women do everything! So, this can be quite different than that of a wife and may tend to lead to conflicts.

When I was growing up, I had my fair share of chores to do around the house. In addition to kitchen duties, I had to do chores outside as well, such as:

mowing the lawn, trimming the hedges, and raking and bagging the debris afterwards.

Today, I'm not big on doing the dishes, but I do them when I need to. We have a dishwasher, but someone still has to load it. And of course, everyone in the house shares this responsibility. But instead, I prefer trimming the rose bushes outside, pulling weeds, and sweeping up the backyard deck. I regularly water the flowerbeds and the grass as well.

So, my husband might think, "Why am I – the man – doing the dishes more than my wife is? Isn't she supposed to be doing that chore?" But he also needs to consider the yard work that I'm doing that he doesn't have to do—or pay someone else to do it. I also need to consider that my husband was raised differently. He was raised in a home where his mom probably cooked and did the dishes. Now that I don't work at a 9 to 5, I have more time to fiddle around in the kitchen in the mornings, while everyone else has to rush off to work. I still have many things to do during the course of my day. But I have more flexibility now, so I am growing to enjoy washing the dishes. It is my kitchen after all, and my daughters always help me out with organizing things!

The way a home should be run when you are married is different from the way a single-parent home is run. That's something that I have had to come to grips with. And it has not been an easy journey for me to change. The experience of having a mom who was both my mother and father means that I watched her making all of the decisions and not having to acquiesce to a male counterpart. If you were raised by a single parent, you have to learn how a two-parent family should function. And that means taking a lot of what you grew up with and throwing it out of the window. That can be extremely hard to do, however, you at least need to have conversations with your husband about how you were raised and how that may affect some of your ways and your views about your role as a wife.

In Titus, chapter 2, the Bible instructs us in this way:

> "...the older women similarly are to be ... teaching what is right and good, so that they may encourage the young women to tenderly love their husbands and their children, to be sensible, pure, makers of a home [where God is honored], good-natured, being subject to their own husbands, so that the word of God will not be dishonored." (Titus 2: 3 –5 AMP)

That passage contains some of the important things that our mothers or grandmothers needed to teach us about being a wife.

But I will be honest, my mom and grandmother only said, "A man is supposed to take care of you!" I was in my early twenties when I realized there weren't a whole lot of men telling me they just could not wait to take care of me.

My mother loved her children very much. She worked hard, she cooked most of the time, and taught us how to take care of the home. But for 13 years of my life, she had no husband, and when she did marry my stepdad, he moved into a home that my mom had purchased on her own. He carried very little weight in my mind, and I definitely did not look at him as being the head of the house simply because he wasn't.

Maybe your mother or grandmother taught you how a wife should treat her husband, or you observed this for yourself firsthand. If so, that's great. What did you learn about being a wife before you became a wife? Did your mother, or some other wise person, give you any advice on how to be a "good wife"? Think of any advice or words of wisdom about being a wife your mother or grandmother might have given you. Maybe an aunt or older sister instructed you. Whatever advice you got, was it good advice, or not-so-good? If it was wise advice, did you remember to follow it? What do you wish they would have shared with you early on that they failed to tell you?

Your Man Needs Some Tender Loving Care

Let's look a little bit closer at verses 4 and 5 of Titus chapter 2. What exactly do these verses say the older women in our lives should have taught us about being a wife?

Verse 4, "…so that they may encourage the young women to tenderly love their husbands…"

What does it mean to "tenderly love" your husband? At this point you might be saying, "I thought the Bible says that the husband is to love his wife and my job is to respect my husband." That's true, and I'm going to get to that in a few more paragraphs. But this is what Titus says the older women should teach the younger women: to tenderly love their husbands. I believe that we find the answer to what that means in Proverbs, where the qualities of the famous Proverbs 31 Woman are detailed:

> "The heart of her husband trusts in her confidently and relies on and believes in her securely, so that he has no lack of [honest] gain or need of [dishonest] spoil.
> *She comforts, encourages, and does him good as long as there is life within her.*"
> (Proverbs 31:11 –12 AMPC, emphasis added)

In the above verses, we see a picture of a relationship where there is complete and total trust on the part of the husband. His wife comforts and encourages him and treats him good all of her life! Wow! In turn, his heart confidently trusts and relies on her. And he does not lack anything good. How do you think he has arrived at this point of trusting, relying, and confidently believing in his wife?

Well, most likely it is because she has shown him that she can be trusted. We should never give our husbands any reason to doubt our trustworthiness or our love for them. If you have ever said anything that was misunderstood or misconstrued by your husband, like you no longer love him, or that he might have reason to doubt your faithfulness, I recommend rectifying that as soon as possible.

In Beth Jones's book *21 Days to a Satisfied Life*, Beth writes, "Trust is a huge issue in marriage. Jealousy, anger, accusation, and suspicion stem from a heart of distrust. Cultivating trust in marriage will bring a great deal of peace and tranquility. How she relates to him is the reason her husband's heart can trust, rely, and believe in her." [1]

Tell Your Man How You *Really* Feel

I realized recently that I had difficulty communicating with my husband how much I love and cherish him. I think most people would agree that men are usually the ones that are known for having this problem, not women. But nonetheless, I had to realize I needed to let go of my fears and inhibitions and communicate my true feelings to him. I came from a family where the women were not the touchy feely type and they didn't go around saying, "I love you!" to their children or to anyone else.

I'm pretty sure this was a way of protecting my feelings, because of past relationships in which I had been hurt. I had no desire to lay all of my cards out and thereby become vulnerable. Don't get me wrong, I have always told my husband that I love him. But I realized that I needed to really tell him how much I love him, and how much he means to me. And I also need to show him this with my actions on a regular basis. But don't worry, I took care of that.

What about you? Take some time to think about how you felt when you first realized you were falling in love with your husband. Next, think about the love you have for him now. You may need to dig deep, past any hurts or disappointments that you may have experienced or may still be holding onto. Write down what you would tell your husband about how much you love him. To get your emotions bubbling to the surface, look a little way down the tunnel as I have sometimes thought of things in the future that you can't see. When you are in a tunnel, you can't see what is at the end of it until you get a little further down.

So think about how you would feel if your husband told you he no longer wanted to be with you because you have not been showing him adequately how much you love and need him. As I read that word need, I want to make myself clear: We do need our husbands, and we want to let them know that we do in fact love them. But we don't want to be needy. There's a difference. Needing your husband's love and presence in your life – because you love him and chose him for all of the reasons that you did—is quite different from being needy. Being needy is when you act as though you can't live without someone or you refuse to give them, and yourself, space necessary to be an individual person.

How would you feel after the anger and after telling him off, etc. Write down how you would feel once you realize you were one day away from losing your best friend and he was on his way out the door bags in hand! What would you say to him? I know you think right now you would be saying, "Bye, sucker! And good riddance!" But look down the tunnel a little bit further to how you are going to feel when you are there at home all alone and knowing you are going to miss this person with whom you have been spending so many years of your life.

How are you going to feel knowing he most likely will not be coming back after he walks out of that door? Someone may have already experienced this feeling when they had no control over the situation. Maybe your husband has already left your home, and you are now separated. Separation is the next step from divorce, so don't play around with taking that route. But if you are separated already, and you are praying and hoping for a reconciliation, I've written a prayer in chapter 2 just for you to pray over your marriage.

Listen, I don't mean that you need to be begging, groveling, or pleading with your husband to stay despite the fact you are unhappy in your marriage. No, in fact, I want you to do just the opposite! I want you to honor yourself, by being honest with yourself about your true feelings, and by reflecting on all of the love and care that you still have for the man that you married. I know, by no means is he perfect. But neither are you! I want you to experience the feeling that I had after I told my husband how much I love him. We need to spend ten times the amount of time we spend focusing on our husband's faults focusing on the reasons why we love them and married them in the first place.

It's a difficult tightrope to walk these days as a wife, because nowadays women take pride in their strength – and not needing a man for anything. But we do need our husbands (for a few things – well maybe a lot of things) *and* we also need to maintain our self-respect and our self-love. I think that you will feel so much better when you tell your husband how much he means to you, and you also may need to apologize for the way that you have been speaking to him, even if you have had good reason. But after that, girlfriend, go say a prayer to the Lord, give it to Him, make yourself something to eat, and do something for yourself!

Also, I cannot stress enough the importance of forgiveness in a marriage. You cannot possibly love

someone to the fullest potential if you are holding on to
unforgiveness for something that they've done, or
something someone else has done. I'm not telling you
that you have to forgive him for something terrible. But
in my experience, much of the time, it was something
small that I needed to forgive my husband for. And it
was just how I kept choosing to view the situation. I
often would just replay something that happened over
and over again in my head. Just choosing to dwell on
the situation—choosing to dwell on the negative – even
when my husband was telling me that it was an
inaccurate view of what happened. In those instances,
you need to cast down those thoughts and imaginations,
like the word commands us in 2 Corinthians 10, verse
5:

> "…casting down arguments and every high
> thing that exalts itself against the knowledge of
> God, bringing every thought into captivity to the
> obedience of Christ."

You might be asking, what if my husband is taking
my love for granted? I deal with that before I end this
chapter, so keep reading.

What If the Thrill Is Gone?

You may be saying at this point, "I'm not sure if I
still do love my husband," or "My love has faded
away." You are not alone in having those thoughts.
Sometimes, husbands may act in certain ways, or they
say things that can influence our feelings of love. I go
into this in depth (and how you can pray about getting
the love back for your husband) in Chapter 6. But I will
say this, if you didn't still love your husband in some
way, you probably wouldn't be reading this book. I

believe that even though things can begin to look really badly between you and your spouse, you can still get down on your knees and ask God - who created the massive heavens and the universe, and who holds all of that together – to help your marriage situation!

Check Yourself Before You Wreck Your Marriage

Minister Amanda E. Dyson, had this to say, "Men don't fall in love with other women, they fall in love with how they feel about themselves when they're with that person." That's something to think about. You wouldn't want some other woman making your husband feel more loved and better about himself than you do, would you? So, if not, start paying attention to the words that you are saying to him and how you are making him *know* that you love and adore him. The fact is, no one loves your husband more than you do. Another woman – the strange woman – as she is called in proverbs, simply "flatters" men. In Proverbs 2, verse 16, it states, "To deliver you from the immoral woman, from the seductress who flatters with her words, ..." So just be aware of that.

Part 5 – A Legitimate Expectation

I would be remiss if I didn't mention how the husband should be acting towards his wife. In Ephesians 5, verse 22, it says that wives should submit to their husbands, as to the Lord. Then verse 24 says for husbands to love their wives, like Christ loved the church, and gave Himself for her. I will be teaching on these verses in chapter three. But right now, let's read Colossians 3, which basically gives the same command to wives, but has some additional instruction for the men:

> "Husbands, love your wives [be
> affectionate and sympathetic with them] and do
> not be harsh or bitter or resentful toward them."
> (Colossians 3:19 AMPC)

Now that sounds like something that we wives all *should* expect from our husbands, because it is right in the Word of God! In chapter 3 of this book, I go into some detail about the things husbands, and wives, should be doing, in accordance with the word of God.

What do we do and how should we act when our husbands are acting unloving or unkind towards us? A natural reaction is to pounce on them, like a cat on her prey. But we are Christian wives, ladies, so we cannot react in the flesh! So, what do we do? Instead of scratching our prey, we need to pray. Go into your prayer closet, or a room where you can talk to God (or kneel beside your bed) and tell God exactly what your husband is doing. Place him in God's hands and ask God to deal with him. Then go take a nice warm bath and think about how God has your back, and how much He loves you (and your husband too).

Begin to confess certain scriptures over your husband – and over yourself – during your prayer time. One such scripture that I read in my devotional Bible recently is:

"Let all that you do be done with love." (1 Corinthians 16:14) The commentary on that day's Bible reading highlighted this verse. It said this, "The key word in this sentence is the word "all." The Bible exhorts us to perform each and every responsibility, whether spiritual, or temporal, in love... The traditional family unit, now under vicious attack from some sources, would immediately be strengthened. Divorce rates and juvenile delinquency would drop..." I am going to make a habit of confessing this over Gordon and me every day, like this, "Lord, I thank You that all that Gordon and I do is done with love, in Jesus' Name. Amen." Wow, I just said it out loud, and it's powerful to speak the word of God!

I realized several years ago how important it was to incorporate scripture into my prayers. There is power in God's Word. So, I have for years found prayers that do exactly that. An excellent book of prayers is *Prayers That Avail Much for Mothers*. I also have the more comprehensive *Prayers That Avail Much*, both by Germaine Copeland. I highly recommend that you get both of these books. Honestly, I cannot see how most wives (and mothers) make it without such resources to help them navigate the rough waters of marriage and family issues, especially in the culture that we live in today!

Additionally, after you've prayed, the time may eventually come when you will need to address valid, biblical expectations with your husband. I cover this in chapter three in the section entitled: Prayerfully Speak Your Peace. I also go in to much detail on this topic in chapter ten. But let me also add this. Sometimes the most effective weapon to use against the times when your husband isn't acting right, is silence! That's right, just get quiet and pray like I said above and just go on with your life. Go somewhere that makes you happy or work on some project that you have been wanting to finish.

If you change your strategy from how you have always reacted, your husband will start trying to figure out exactly what is going through your mind. You'll put a few things on *his* mind. Sometimes, it's nice to change up. Stop with the fussing and don't let what he's doing upset you. Talk to God about it! God will take care of it.

I have found one of the best things I did was to let go of most of my expectations from my husband that I had been worrying myself silly about. It was near my birthday and very close to Mother's Day. Hubby had been saying stuff like he wasn't going to do this, that, and the other for me. He was saying it jokingly, but I wasn't up for the jokes, so I wrote my husband a note one evening. I told him he didn't have to do anything for me. I said, you don't have to do this, this, and that, etc. No worries. What I was saying with that note was, "Cool! I will stop worrying about and acting like I need you to do anything for me. I am good. I have no expectations."

All I can say is I got one of the most heartfelt responses I've ever gotten from my husband, and basically had one of the best Mother's Day and birthday celebrations I had had in a very long time. I ended up sending him a text on that Monday after my birthday weekend, thanking him for how special, loved, and appreciated I had felt. And I also thanked all of my children who had joined in and helped make my days so special!

What if you feel – even after you've prayed – that something your husband has done or said has affected you so that you can't sleep in the same bed with him that night? Pray about it and if you still feel like you won't be able to sleep next to him, go and sleep in another bedroom, if you have one. But if the Holy Spirit tells you to go ahead and sleep in your marriage bed, please be obedient! Sleep where you are going to get the best rest. Forgive your husband and get your sleep!

Chapter Two

Why is My Marriage Under Attack?

"The thief comes only to steal and kill and destroy; I have come that they may have life, and have it to the full." (John 10:10 NIV)

Part 1 – The Enemy's Initiative
Satan Is a Thief

Have you ever wondered how you can just be minding your own business and things just fall apart? You woke up happy and everything was well between you and your husband. Then for some reason, before the end of the day, it seems like all hell has broken loose. You and hubby are fighting, one or both of you starts cursing, and you say something terribly awful to either him, your kids, or both. You just wish you could take it all back.

Well, what has happened right in front of your eyes, is Satan, the thief, just came in and stole from you. He stole your peace, tranquility, and joy. He wants to destroy your marriage and your whole family and leave you not even remembering how it all started! If you're not careful, that's exactly what he will get away with, especially if you don't recognize that it's him and do something about it. Something we must do in these situations is take authority. Speak the name of Jesus—the Name at which every knee must eventually bow—and pray!

On a few occasions, I have experienced what I have just described. And I had to go into my prayer closet and begin to pray and ask for God's help in the situation. I will go into more detail about what the specific components of your prayer need to be in Part 3 of this chapter.

In John 10:10, the scripture that starts this chapter, Jesus warns us that the devil is a robber, and he comes to destroy things. But Jesus finishes the sentence with the promise that His mission is to give us life, and a rich one at that!

Kicked Out of Heaven

Something I realized shortly after I got married was that one of the devil's primary targets for creating havoc and destruction is in marriages – especially Christian ones. The scriptures tell us in Isaiah 14 that Satan was an angel of light and his ejection from Heaven's domain was due to his desire to be like God.

> "How you are fallen from heaven, O Lucifer, son of the morning! How you are cut down to the ground, you who weakened the nations! For you have said in your heart: 'I will ascend into heaven, I will exalt my throne above the stars of God; I will also sit on the mount of the congregation on the farthest sides of the north; I will ascend above the heights of the clouds, I will be like the Most High.' Yet you

shall be brought down to Sheol, To the lowest depths of the Pit." (Isaiah 14: 12-15)

Because of Satan's continuous covetousness of God's position and His creations, one of the manifestations is his demonic influence on marriages everywhere. We know from Genesis 1 that God created marriage and then called it "very good."

> "So, God created man in His own image; in the image of God He created him; male and female He created them. Then God blessed them…Then God saw everything that He had made, and indeed it was very good. So, the evening and the morning were the sixth day." (Genesis 1: 27- 28,31)

Because of Satan's downright disdain for God's role as Creator, and how He designed the beautiful symbiotic relationship between a man and his wife, Satan has made many attempts to downgrade, hijack, or outright destroy God's wonderful creation of marriage. This is also why we see such a move in the area of counterfeit marriages between same sex individuals.

Part 2 – The Enemy's Influence in Media & Marriage
Prince of the Airwaves

In Ephesians 2: 2, Satan is called the "prince of the power of the air, the spirit that now worketh in the children of disobedience." Television, radio, and even the internet are all transmitted through use of the airwaves within the earth's atmosphere. Perhaps you have noticed that there seems to be some evil influences in the television and movie industry? Just look at how demonic the horror movies are. It has become very difficult to even watch a television program without something gross, wicked, blatantly sexual, or violent popping up in a scene – seemingly unrelated to the plot at times.

Television depicts marriage as a miserable arrangement. And motion picture studios are always feeding their audiences with symbols of adultery, divorce, and violence in marriage, even murder.

The Top 5 TV Influencers

According to "The 50 Most Definitive Family TV Shows, Ranked" (vulture.com, Jan.2018, accessed August 21, 2021), the following family television shows are ranked in the top five: *The Simpsons, All in the Family, Roseanne, The Cosby Show*, and *Married... with Children*.

Out of these top five ranked T.V. shows, it is probably *The Simpsons*, and of course, *The Cosby Show* that gave the best portrayal of the wife. According to the article in vulture.com: *All in the Family's* Archie Bunker has a "... good-hearted, 'dingbat' wife Edith,"... "Roseanne takes the oh-so-wholesome role of TV mom and turns her into someone who occasionally gets too drunk and whose teenagers have real problems;" and the article states that *Married... with Children's* Al Bundy is the "bitter, emasculated father (who) call(s) his wife a money-grubbing ditz and his teenage daughter a slut." Do you think it's just a coincidence that the two male chauvinists' initials are both "A.B.," and they respectively called their beloved wives, "dingbat" and "ditz"? I think not!

Despite the lows that *Married...with Children* achieved with respect to its portrayal of the American family, the article on Vulture.com said, "For better or worse (probably worse), this is one of the most influential shows ever made." That says a lot about the negative influence Satan has had on marriages and families through many of the television shows piped into our living rooms every week!

With so much junk out there calling itself "entertainment" available for your viewing pleasure, it would be beneficial to try to limit the amount of television you may be watching. I recommend fasting from TV periodically for a few days during the week. I have done fasts from television, and I learned just how addicted I was. I still struggle with wanting to just turn the darn thing on sometimes. Now, I try to only watch television on the weekends or holidays, especially when I am writing. But if family is visiting, or the NBA finals or on, the television will definitely be on a lot. I do enjoy watching cooking shows on YouTube, while I'm making dinner sometimes. But I am learning how relaxing and uplifting it is to just listen to Christian music while I'm in the kitchen cooking.

I'm not saying there aren't some really good shows on television, as well as some really positive portrayals of marriage and family life. *The Cosby Show*, for one, was extremely positive in that it was one of the first to show a Black family in which the mom and dad were both professionals and the family was just as normal as any other. And there are other shows as well – great shows that are appropriate for the whole family to watch.

However, there are many other television shows

that are not appropriate to watch for anyone calling themselves a Christian. Keep in mind, you are exposing your kids to these programs as well. You may think the kids aren't paying attention, or they don't know what you're watching in your bedroom, but they know, believe me. I taught middle school for 17 years and high school for 4, and I know kids are aware of and imitate everything their parents listen to and watch.

You might say that I'm being somewhat of a downer about this subject of the media. However, in Psalms 103, David made a vow to God. He said:

"I will be careful to live a blameless life—
when will you come to help me?
I will lead a life of integrity in my own home. I
will refuse to look at anything vile and vulgar. I
hate all who deal crookedly; I will have nothing
to do with them.
I will reject perverse ideas and stay away from
every evil." (Psalm 101: 2 – 4 NLT)

The New Testament also admonishes us:
"Do not be unequally yoked together with
unbelievers. For what fellowship has
righteousness with lawlessness? And
what communion has light with darkness?" (2
Corinthians 6:14)

The second scripture is usually applied to marrying someone who isn't a believer, but what you should remember is that most of the producers and directors in Hollywood must not be Christians in any way, shape, or form. If you observe closely, Christianity and Christians are mostly portrayed in a negative light in movies and television. Hollywood portrays us as not that smart, overly religious, pious, hypocritical sinners, or just downright evil people. So, when you bring the creative works of unbelievers into your home, not only are you pumping yourself and your family with their negativity about your faith, but you are also fellowshipping with unbelievers, by allowing their belief systems in as well.

The Impact of Media on Husbands & Wives

Couples, either together or watching programs separately, need to be really careful about what they are viewing on television. Why is this? Television and movies are very powerful tools for introducing thoughts and fantasies that are just plain unrealistic into our minds. It's interesting how television and movies often romanticize dating relationships and then vilify marital relationships. The danger there is, wives watch romantic movies and then want to make comparisons to their own real-life relationships, based on something that is written in a script. Or they watch some show where the husband is cheating, and then they may begin to suspect their own husband of cheating. Wives can also watch a movie about a bad marriage or a bad husband and then start seeing a connection between what they just viewed in the movie, and what may or may not be happening in their own marriage. Bad idea. Do not do this, please.

And "reality TV shows" definitely are not real. They are scripted. The plots have way too much drama and foul language, and the people involved don't seem to need to work to make a living. The latter is definitely not realistic.

The risk for husbands is that there seems to be so

many overly sexual scenes and underdressed females (and males) on the TV screen, that it is almost tantamount to pornography. There are a lot of programs and movies that a Christian man, married or single, just should not be partaking of—period. If you notice this is an issue with your husband watching these types of shows, pray about it first, and speak to your husband about it when you get a well-timed opportunity to do so. Let him know those shows are just not appropriate for either of you to be watching, and he should consider watching other shows. There are many others he could choose.

If your husband is watching actual pornography, try to get Christian counseling. I cannot give you advice on this topic, as I have not experienced this problem in my marriage. I can only recommend that your husband get help, and that you pray for him. You may want to get the book *The Power of A Praying Wife* by Stormie Omartian. Especially look at the prayer on page 75 entitled "His Temptations."

If you have been watching inappropriate television movies or shows with an inordinate amount of sex, violence, and foul language, I advise you to just stop now! Believe me when I tell you, it will only cause problems in the end in some way!

If you get resistance from your husband about the shows he's watching, just continue to pray about it. Bind those kinds of shows away from your husband in your prayers and loose the power of God over him to break every stronghold (Matthew 18:18). You can even confess Psalm 101, verses 2 – 4 that you just read above, over your husband. Just insert his name, instead of "I." In the meantime, definitely don't let it bother you, and don't get jealous about him looking at shows with scantily clothed women. This really used to bother me in the past. My husband would be watching something, and I would walk in the room just at the moment when some sex scene was on the screen. I would become very insecure inside, and I would mostly just walk right back out of the room.

Even if we were watching a movie that had a good-looking actress in it, I would feel insecure in some ways. But actually, I have also noticed lately that my husband does not just sit there all goo-goo-eyed watching the pretty women on television. He will turn and look at me – his beautiful and fabulous wife – who is right there in the room with him! I have worked on my self-esteem and my view of myself now. And I don't let the pretty actresses on the screens bother me anymore. I'm working on myself – going to the gym, getting my exercise, taking vitamins, and making sure I eat a healthy diet. There are pretty women everywhere. That's why it's best to keep ourselves looking the very best. I'll speak more about this in chapter four.

Part 3 – The Enemy's Interference Coming from Within

Interference is not restricted to outside influences such as the media. Demonic influences can reach right into your mind and emotions and have a profound effect on your relationship with your spouse. Jesus said, in order to be a follower of Him, you must deny your own selfish desires and "take up your cross daily" (Luke 9:23). We must "die" to, or say "no" to, our own weaknesses that cause us to sin. We must deliberately put Jesus Christ in the center of our daily lives and marriages through prayer, reading the Bible, and continual surrender to God's will, in order to be victorious over the devil's attacks.

Pastor Michael Todd says something about this on day 16 of his book *Relationship Goals Challenge – 30 Days from Good to Great*. In the chapter entitled "Go to the Manufacturer," he says a lot of people in romantic relationships are suffering from problems that existed years before the start of their relationships. He writes, "There's an anger problem. There's a commitment problem. There are bad habits of laziness or put-downs or lack of confidence...it's good for people to recognize they're dealing with a problem like this, but they've also got to deal with it in a way that's helpful to them and their relationship, not making things worse." In his book, and in this chapter mentioned, he emphasizes the importance of going to God to help you work through the problems that you or your spouse may be having, since only God is aware of the intricacies of our makeup deep within.

What are some of the sinful actions and behaviors that can rear their ugly heads and try to throw a wrench in your marriage? Some of the big ones that may come to mind might be adultery or cheating, drug and alcohol problems, and spouses being physically and emotionally abusive. However, some of the most common problems in marriages are strife and anger. We can look to God, and His word to help us in these areas.

Many people have anger problems, as Pastor Todd mentioned. Where does the anger come from? An article entitled "Dealing with Anger in Marriage" by Cornerstone Marriage and Family Ministries (marriageministries.org, n.d., accessed on August 30,

2021), starts with these words:

> "During my 24 years of working with couples in distressed marriages, I would say that anger is among the top, most prevalent issues couples face in their marriages. About one third of clients are dealing with anger in their relationships. I think most counselors would agree anger is one of the most prevalent contributors to the demise of marital relationships today."

The article goes on to say,
> "… Though anger is an emotion common to all of us, few people are naturally skilled at being able to control this unruly emotion in healthy ways so that it does not become an emotional threat to our spouse and children. Most of us rely on a few specific ways of dealing with our anger that we learned as children and took with us into adulthood. These "inherited" ways of dealing with anger in marriage often have a destructive impact upon ourselves and upon those closest to us. Recognizing what makes us angry can help us find better ways to cope with this emotion."

This is an excellent article, and I highly recommend reading it in its entirety, if your spouse – or maybe even you, have episodes of anger in your relationship. I like that the article addresses the impact of anger in marriage, provides a quick test you can take, and provides scriptural guidance as well as recommendations on the topic.

As I mentioned in the beginning of this chapter, sometimes something – mostly insignificant – can just happen, and you or your spouse will react with anger. I have reacted to something my husband did and became angry. I've experienced my sleep being affected because I was upset, and there he was just sleeping and snoring! This is not worth me making my heart beat faster, and so forth.

The Importance of Prayer

Throughout this chapter, you've noticed I've mentioned prayer a lot. You must go into your prayer closet and pray. Oftentimes, you may not even want to pray simply because you are so mad! You may even feel (and actually be) justified at being angry with your mate. This is exactly where the devil wants you to be, because then he is able to do his work of separation.

You can't let the adversary of your soul win in any aspect of your life! You have got to get up off that sofa, or out of that bed, and get down on your knees. I like to go literally into my closet because it is quiet and there are no distractions. I feel I can hear from God better. But kneeling beside your bed, or right where you are, you can begin to pray to God and ask Him to take control of the situation. You can even type the prayer out on the note's app on your cell phone if you're not at home. I can almost guarantee you God will work out the situation if you just tell Him what happened. I know, He already knows, but tell Him, nonetheless. And also, ask God to intervene and help you and your husband to make amends.

Do you know how to pray in the Spirit? Then do it at times like these. If you do not know about praying in the Spirit, read the Book of Acts. Another thing that is always beneficial to have, is a prayer book with pre-written prayers arranged by topic. The prayers need to be scripture-based. The book can also be one of those that has potential areas of need at the top of each page, and then gives several applicable scriptures to read. I like to read the prayers or the scriptures, out loud and personalize them by saying "I," or "we," or inserting my husband's and/or my name. The Word will strengthen you in your inner man and so will praying in the Spirit. After speaking God's Word, and praying in the Spirit, you will be able to boldly take authority over the situation and continue to pray for your marriage, your home, and your family with the authority that is in the name of Jesus Christ. And you need to bind Satan away from your marriage, loose him from his assignment in your marriage, and then loose God's power over your marriage, like it says in Matthew 18:18. The following prayer was given to me by the Holy Spirit:

> "Father God, I come before You Lord humbly, but yet boldly, because You said that I can come boldly before Your thrown of Grace, that I may obtain mercy and find grace to help me in time of need. Lord, You said in Your word, to ask, and it will be given to me, seek, and I will find. I ask You to intervene in the situation that has occurred between me and _____ (husband's name). Lord, You already know, but this is what happened:

_____
_____.

"Father God, I know that You are able to do exceedingly and abundantly above all that I can ever ask or imagine, according to the power that is at work within me. And I know that You love us. I ask You Lord to turn this situation around and make everything alright in our marriage, in Your Son Jesus' Name. Lord, You said that whatever we bind on earth, You will bind it in heaven. And whatever we loose on earth, You will loose it in heaven. So, Lord, in accordance with Your Word, I bind and stand up against all the schemes and the strategies and the deceits of the devil. I bind the devil AWAY from me, my husband, my marriage, and my family RIGHT NOW, in Your Son Jesus Christ's Name! And I thank You Father God that You bind the devil away from my marriage and away from my family, in heaven. Lord, I loose the devil from his assignment against me, against my husband, my marriage, and my family, in Jesus' Name, right now. I thank You Heavenly Father for loosing the devil from his assignment against us. Lord, I loose Your heavenly power over me, over my husband, my marriage, and my family, in Jesus' Name, right now. I thank You Heavenly Father for loosing Your power and control over us! I ask You Lord to move swiftly to reunite my husband and I in love and fellowship and in one accord, in Your Son's Mighty Name I pray, AMEN!"

What I have given you is a strategy to attack almost any problem that you may come up against. But I almost left out, praise. Thanking God and praising

Him helps bring forth victory. And the following word of scripture has really helped me:

> "So I pray for you Gentiles that God who gives you hope will keep you happy and full of peace as you believe in him. I pray that God will help you overflow with hope in him through the Holy Spirit's power within you." (Romans 15: 13 TLB)

The Sins of the Flesh and The Fruit of the Spirit

Here is a list of sinful behaviors upon which we all need to review and reflect. Honestly do some soul searching. Pray and ask God to reveal if you suffer from any of these. The second list – the fruit of the Spirit – should be the qualities we pray to exemplify on a regular basis. We can also meditate on and memorize the verses from the Bible that help us get rid of bad behaviors and achieve the good ones. Let's look at Galatians 5:

> "Now the **practices of the sinful nature** are *clearly* evident: they are **sexual immorality**, **impurity**, **sensuality** (total irresponsibility, lack of self-control), **idolatry**, **sorcery**, **hostility**, **strife**, **jealousy**, **fits of anger**, **disputes**, **dissensions**, **factions** [that promote heresies], **envy**, **drunkenness**, **riotous behavior**, and *other* things like these. I warn you beforehand, just as I did previously, that those who practice such things will not inherit the kingdom of God. But the **fruit of the Spirit** [the result of His presence within us] is **love**

[unselfish concern for others], **joy**, [inner] **peace**, **patience** [not the ability to wait, but how we act while waiting], **kindness**, **goodness**, **faithfulness**, **gentleness**, **self-control**. Against such things there is no law. And those who belong to Christ Jesus have crucified the sinful nature together with its passions and appetites." (Galatians 5: 19 – 24 AMP, emphasis added)

You may have noticed the passage is addressed to those who *practice* the sinful behaviors. It is they who will not inherit the kingdom of God. This is referring to someone who willfully and deliberately continues to commit these sins, even without repentance or feeling contrite or sorry for their actions. When you were saved—or you asked Jesus to come into your heart, and You acknowledged Him as the Son of God—Jesus instantly came to abide with you and so did the Holy Spirit. Therefore, if you do something that is of the flesh, or sinful, the Holy Spirit will let you know and you will feel convicted about your actions. Your response should be to immediately repent and ask for God's forgiveness, in Jesus' name. This may happen over and over again, but at some point, you should be able to get the victory over this problem with recurring sinful behavior.

For example, let's say you have a problem with constantly wanting to start arguments with your husband (strife), or vice versa, maybe your husband has this problem. First of all, you need to look up as many verses of scripture you can find that deal with strife. Proverbs is loaded with verses that speak about the contentious wife and controlling your tongue. I make it a habit of trying to read something from the book of Proverbs every day. Also, Ephesians states:

> "Let all bitterness and wrath and anger and clamor [perpetual animosity, resentment, strife, fault-finding] and slander be put away from you, along with every kind of malice [all spitefulness, verbal abuse, malevolence]. Be kind *and* helpful to one another, tender-hearted [compassionate, understanding], forgiving one another [readily and freely], just as God in Christ also forgave you." (Ephesians 4: 31 – 32 AMP)

An Example of a Scripture – Based Prayer
This above scripture is an example of one into which you can insert your husband's and your names and make a prayer out of it. Like this:

> "Lord, I ask You to help
> _____ (husband's name) and me to let all bitterness and wrath and anger and clamor [perpetual animosity, resentment, strife, fault-finding] and slander… be put away from us, right now, along with every kind of malice [all spitefulness, verbal abuse, or malevolence]. I ask You Lord to show us how to be kind and helpful to one another, tenderhearted [compassionate and understanding]. Lord, show
> _____ and me how to be forgiving of each other [readily and freely], just as God in Christ forgave us." After saying the prayer in this way, you can then make it a confession, by

saying, "Lord, I *thank You for* helping...
instead of, "Lord, *I ask You to*...."

Prior to praying the above scripture prayer, you may want to just talk to God about the problem you and your spouse are having, and how hard it is for you to stop the problem. Let Him show you where it all started. Also, beware of constantly finding fault with your husband, as this is not what we need to be doing as wives. We need to be building our husbands up, supporting them when we are needed to do so, and honoring him with our words and actions.

I want you to take a long look at your husband. Stop looking at what he does all of the time and look at him! What do you truly see? Do you see someone who is tired from working himself to the bone and needs you to arrange for a nice weekend getaway? Or do you perhaps see someone who needs you to do something simple that he needs. You may see a man who's being ripped apart on his job by an unforgiving and hard-to-please boss. Or maybe you see a man who just needs you to quietly be by his side, and just "be" with him. Stop complaining, blaming, and fussing. The book of Proverbs states that it is better to live on the corner of a rooftop, than in a sprawling mansion with a quarrelsome wife (Proverbs 21:9).

Lastly, if your husband is the one who gets angry or argues with you habitually, then you need to know it is not God's will for you to stand there and listen to him screaming, being angry, or just being confrontational. The Bible says, "Make no friendship with an angry man, and with a furious man do not go, lest you learn his ways and set a snare for your soul" (Proverbs 22:24

– 25).

Let him know you are not going to participate in his argument, his yelling, or his angry outbursts. You will need to physically walk away and let him know you will pray that you two have more civilized conversations. What you are really going to be doing is praying and binding that anger away from your husband, praying for his communication skills to improve (Matthew 18:18). Hence, the prayer that I just went over earlier.

You may also need to bring in reinforcements in the form of someone that you can really trust to pray in agreement with you and not just spread your business (see Matthew 18:19-20). You may want to seriously consider getting a prayer partner, even if it's you who has the sinful problem. There's more power when two, or even three, agree.

I do need to interject here that oftentimes we wives can be guilty of igniting the fire underneath our hubbies' feet with the words we say or deliver at inappropriate times. Do not start serious conversations when your husband is either tired, hungry, ready to go to bed, or experiencing times of job-related stress. And definitely don't expect him to be receptive to your grave concerns if you haven't made love in a while.

Part 4 – The Enemy's Achilles Heel (How to Beat Him at His Game)

Stand Firm Against the Enemy

We must be aware and alert to the devil's strategies and tactics. Listen to what the Bible tells us, in the book of First Peter:

"Be careful—watch out for attacks from

Satan, your great enemy. He prowls around like a hungry, roaring lion, looking for some victim to tear apart. Stand firm when he attacks. Trust the Lord; and remember that other Christians all around the world are going through these sufferings too." (1 Peter 5: 8- 9 TLB)

Through regular prayer and studying the Word of God, you can anticipate ways the enemy will attempt to attack our marriage relationship. We also must be ready to stand firm against him as stated in the above text. The Bible says to resist the devil and he will flee (James 4:7). The Message translation puts it like this:

"So let God work his will in you. Yell a loud *no* to the Devil and watch him make himself scarce. Say a quiet *yes* to God and he'll be there in no time. Quit dabbling in sin. Purify your inner life. Quit playing the field. Hit bottom and cry your eyes out. The fun and games are over. Get serious, really serious. Get down on your knees before the Master; it's the only way you'll get on your feet" (James 4: 7 – 10 MSG).

Satan Is a Liar
Satan uses lies and deception to get couples to focus on the negative instead of on the blessings God has for their marriage. Why does he do this? And how is he such a master mind at it?

First let's deal with the why. In the beginning of this chapter, I gave you one reason why Satan attacks marriages – because he is covetous of what God made.

But there is also another reason he is so bent on trying to destroy Christian marriages in particular and that is because of the calling and purpose each one of us has, and how we can shine a light into this dark world that may help to bring others to know Jesus. If the devil can keep Christian husbands and wives constantly in a state of disagreement, or just even in a state of distrust or indifference, then he's able to keep them from doing the kingdom work God planned for them to do.

Very early on, when Gordon and I first got married, I started going to a certain convalescent home that was not far from our church. I would take my karaoke box and microphone, and sing for the patients. At some point, Gordon started going with me. We would also go to some of the patients' rooms and pray for them. This was only the start of what God had planned for us to do together. Later we were chosen to become the new co-chairs of the couples' ministry at our church, Trinity Baptist.

Then before our first daughter was born, we both were very active in the Music Ministry. I sang in the Young Adult Choir – the choir traveled every year to minister out of state, and we had an annual concert that was amazing— and Gordon was the audio person who set up all of the microphones and operated the sound system. He also recorded the services and ran the church's tape ministry. After that, he served on the board of trustees to help with the selection of the new pastor. When we eventually moved our membership and joined Cottonwood Church, we served together in the Visitor's Lounge ministry. In between serving at those two churches, we also attended Power Christian Center and were extremely involved there as well.

But there have been a few seasons in which the devil tried his best to throw wrenches in our relationship and get one of us to call it quits. If it had not been for the faithfulness of God, in answering our prayers and the prayers of family members – along with our decision to commit to being obedient to His plan for our lives – our marriage and our service to others certainly would have experienced a different outcome.

Now let's get to how the devil works his strategies of deception. Jesus said that Satan is the father of all lies. In John, Jesus says,

> "He ... does not stand in the truth, because there is no truth in him. When he speaks a falsehood, he speaks what is natural to him, for he is a liar [himself] and the father of lies *and* of all that is false. (John 8:44 AMPC)

If our enemy, the devil, can get you to believe a lie about your relationship or about your husband, he's planted a seed that can destroy your marriage.

Let's take for example a hypothetical situation. Let's say that you haven't been feeling like your husband has been paying enough attention to you lately, or he seems to always be looking at his cell phone when he's around you. Then you end up watching *Cheaters* on television. The next thing you know, the devil whispers an allegation in your perked up little ears accusing your husband of cheating on you. Then, you start setting your mind on the idea that he must be interested in another woman. You attach his changed behavior to Satan's suggestion. You wonder, *why else is he acting differently? Oh yes, and that has to be why he's always looking at his phone.* Before you know it, you're going through his phone while he's asleep – missing out on your rest – or you start an argument with him. Guess what? This is all the devil's doing, and he's accomplished what he wants. Hubby's now sleeping on the couch, or you're mad and decide to sleep in the guest bedroom, or he stormed out and left completely because he just wants to come home to peace and not be put on trial when he walks in the house.

The Green-Eyed Monster Called Jealousy

The example that I have detailed above is just one scenario of how you can allow lies to occupy your mind and motivate you to do dumb things in your marriage. I can definitely speak about this problem of letting negative and distrustful thoughts affect my actions because I've been the poster child for allowing that to occur at one point in my marriage. Being sucked into this trick of the devil had everything to do with insecurities within myself.

The example situation I gave above also involves jealousy, and I have been held hostage by that terrible emotion in the past as well. At the root of jealousy is a lack of a positive self- esteem and a lack of the knowledge of how jealousy is so-not-worth the time you can put into it. Jealousy in relationships is a desire to control someone and can be very dangerous to your health.

First of all, you cannot control anyone but (hopefully) yourself! You nor I will ever be able to control our husbands. And heaven forbid if we should be able to do so! Further, jealousy involves too much energy. The Bible says jealousy also is rottenness to the bones. I want to give you a few different translations of this verse to help you if you have jealous tendencies:

"A calm *and* undisturbed mind *and* heart are the life *and* health of the body, but envy, jealousy, *and* wrath are like rottenness of the bones." (Proverbs 14:30 AMPC)

"A peaceful heart leads to a healthy body; jealousy is like cancer in the bones." (NLT)

"A heart at peace gives life to the body, but envy rots the bones." (NIV)

Do Some Self-Inventory

Periodically, take an inventory of the self-talk you are saying or allowing to be repeated within your mind. Take some time this week and begin to write down some of the statements or thoughts going on inside of your head. What are some of the thoughts or scenarios you think about when it comes to your self-image, your husband, and your relationship? Once you have taken some time to survey the things you are saying about yourself, your husband, what he may be doing or thinking, and where you believe your relationship may be headed, ask yourself what truth or actual events these thoughts are based upon. We have to get to a place where we make sure we are seeing ourselves and our husbands the way God sees us!

God's word is the first truth we should look at. Next, look at actual events that you have seen openly and clearly with your own eyes. Stop trying to read your husband's mind or interjecting your own opinion or slant to the reality of what actually happened. You do have every right to be secure in your marriage, but insecurities based upon misplaced suppositions will not make you more comfortable in your relationship.

Forgive and Trust God

Jealousy in relationships can also be a result of a person distrusting their spouse. Maybe you have caught your husband in a lie. Or maybe he told you a lie, or withheld something important from you, and then told you the truth at some point. Was he profoundly sorry for his deception or omission of the truth? Maybe he was afraid he would lose you if he told you the truth about himself? This is what happened in my marriage. My husband had a son prior to even meeting me. I think he knew I felt very strongly about not wanting to have any children outside of my marriage, because it would involve having another woman in our lives. So, he withheld that very important piece of information from me for years after we got married.

Sometimes, the reason why people do disconcerting things is because of some other issue or problem they have going on deep down inside. We can't seem to understand why or how they could have done those things, but they might not know either. Now I understand my husband's not revealing this secret to me was more because he just didn't have the ability to communicate it. He didn't know what to say and he probably knew it was going to be a point of contention between us, so he simply avoided the conversation all together. Combine that fact with my infertility issues during the first five years of marriage, and that led to the duration of him not wanting to tell me the problem definitely wasn't him.

The fact that he didn't tell me he had a son, and his tendency to not communicate, led me later on in our marriage to often wonder if he was withholding other things from me. How much did he still love me after 20 years of marriage? He would always give me beautiful cards that said how much he loved and appreciated me, but not much of this did he say verbally. Therefore, I went through a time – especially after I turned fifty – when I was practically a mad woman trying to figure out what he may have been withholding from me.

You may wonder if you can really trust your husband. I have come to understand that it's better to trust and believe in your mate, than to distrust and always be full of doubt and disbelief. You probably know your husband better than most anyone else does. After all, you have lived with him 24/7 for x- number of years straight. You have slept by his side, made love to him, and seen him at his worst. What do you see in your husband? Remember the good you saw in him when you first married him. I truly believe the passing of time tries to steal away from us the essence of what is inside of us. We can get so hung up on the current problems and situations, that we forget what brought us together and all that we've been through over the years together. Remember the happy times, the milestones you accomplished together. Recall the things you accomplished only because you did them together.

Putting On the Whole Armor of God

With Satan ever on the attack, it is vitally important to be protected by the whole armor of God in order to withstand his attacks. As you read this, imagine you are a soldier, and you've got to get dressed for your battle. You must make sure not to forget any piece of your gear so you can effectively defend yourself, your family, and your marriage from the devil's strategies.

1)   First, stand, and gird your loins about with

truth. (Ephesians 6:14)
To gird all around, means to fasten one's
belt on. In a soldier's armor, your belt has
two metal plates that hang down and
protect your loins from getting injured. In
the spiritual armor, this is symbolic of
girding your loins with truth, integrity, and
courage.

2) Second, put on the breastplate of
righteousness, or the thick armor that would
protect your chest and heart from being
injured. (6:14)
Your breastplate is the righteousness that
comes from being in right standing with
God, through your faith in Christ.

3) Third, put on your army shoes or boots, that
are actually made from the Gospel of peace
– which is the Good News. (6:15)
That means that knowing the good news
that Christ reined victorious against Satan
thousands of years ago, makes us able to
walk in peace and confidence during any
attempted attack of the enemy.

4) Next, pick up your shield that is able to
deflect the flaming arrows (or even bullets)
that are shot at you.
That shield is your faith in the Word of
God, which is able to quench (or put out)
all the fiery darts of the wicked one. (6:16)

5) Now fasten the helmet of salvation on your
head – it is your salvation in Christ. (6:17)
Your head is the most important part of
your body, and yet this verse says your

head is protected because of your salvation through Jesus Christ.

6) Finally, take the sword of the Spirit, which is the word of God! (6:17) Speak the word out of your mouth just like Jesus did when He was in the wilderness being tempted by the devil! We must pray and confess the Word of God over ourselves, our mates, and our marriages. Then, we will get the victory! Hallelujah!

Now, let's read verses 10 through 18 together:

"In conclusion, be strong in the Lord [draw your strength from Him and be empowered through your union with Him] and in the power of His [boundless] might. Put on the full armor of God [for His precepts are like the splendid armor of a heavily armed soldier], so that you may be able to [successfully] stand up against all the schemes *and* the strategies *and* the deceits of the devil. For our struggle is not against flesh and blood [contending only with physical opponents], but against the rulers, against the powers, against the world forces of this [present] darkness, against the spiritual *forces* of wickedness in the heavenly (supernatural) *places*. Therefore, put on the complete armor of God, so that you will be able to [successfully] resist *and* stand your ground in the evil day [of danger], and having done everything [that the crisis demands], to stand firm [in your place, fully prepared, immovable, victorious]. So, stand firm *and* hold your ground, HAVING TIGHTENED THE WIDE BAND OF TRUTH (personal integrity, moral courage) AROUND

YOUR WAIST and HAVING PUT ON THE BREASTPLATE OF
RIGHTEOUSNESS (an upright heart), and having strapped
on YOUR FEET THE GOSPEL OF PEACE IN PREPARATION [to
face the enemy with firm-footed stability and the
readiness produced by the good news]. Above all, lift
up the [protective] shield of faith with which you can
extinguish all the flaming arrows of the evil *one*. And
take THE HELMET OF SALVATION, and the sword of the
Spirit, which is the Word of God. With all prayer and
petition pray [with specific requests] at all times [on
every occasion and in every season] in the Spirit, and
with this in view, stay alert with all perseverance and
petition [interceding in prayer] for all God's
people." (Ephesians 6: 10 – 18 AMP)

TANIA CHAPMAN SCOTT

Chapter Three

"God, Is *This* What You Had in Mind?"
Part 1 – Husbands Should Love, Protect, and Cherish Their Wives

My husband Gordon once told me, "God gave Adam a job before he gave him a wife." Let's talk about that.

I believe God made man with an inherent desire to work and be a provider. Most men are driven by a desire to find work. And in their line of work or business, they are able to find much fulfillment. This does not mean you will not need to work as well. Some husbands will feel like they want their wives to work and help out with the expenses while others may want their wives to work in the home. Either way, being a husband is a big responsibility, and they really need to accept that responsibility: to protect and provide for their wife and family.

If you are working, you may even be making more money than your husband does at some point in the marriage. But your husband should be doing some type of work to pitch in for the major expenses such as the house note or the rent, his car note, insurances, etc. That was my number one criterion when I prayed for a husband. I wanted a husband who went to work every day! God definitely answered my prayer, as Gordon is a hard worker.

The Bible says if a man or woman does not work (in some capacity or another) they should not eat. It also says in Ephesians 5 that husbands are to love their wives the same way that Christ loved the church. And since Christ gave His life for the church, that involved some very hard work and sacrifice!

> "Husbands, love your wives [seek the highest good for her and surround her with a caring, unselfish love], just as Christ also loved the church and gave Himself up for her, so that He might sanctify the church, having cleansed her by the washing of water with the word [of God], so that [in turn] He might present the church to Himself in glorious splendor, without spot or wrinkle or any such thing; but that she would be holy [set apart for God] and blameless. Even so husbands should and are morally obligated to love their own wives as [being in a sense] their own bodies. He who loves his own wife loves himself. *For no one ever hated his own body, but [instead] he nourishes and protects and cherishes it*, just as Christ does the church, (Ephesians 5:25-28 AMP) Emphasis added

That is the first design I believe God had in mind for marriages. God designed the man to love his wife and give himself for her, and to be the head of his family, just like Christ is the head of His Church. Men should take responsibility for covering the home. If your husband doesn't work, or has problems finding or keeping a job, you need to pray for him and encourage him regularly. Don't put him down, but instead build him up and ask God to bless him with the job that He has for him. God answers prayer and He is a faithful God.

I still remember more than 20 years ago when I prayed for Gordon as he was interviewing for the job he has right now. I still pray for him on his job. I pray this short prayer frequently:

> "Lord, I pray that You will establish the works of Gordon's hands. I pray that You will continue to give him favor with those who he reports to, those who report to him, and those who work side-by-side with him."

Pray that your husband will be well paid for the work he does, and that he finds much fulfillment and joy in his job. There is an excellent prayer in Stormie Omartian's book *The Power of A Praying Wife* called "His Work." I confess that prayer over Gordon on a regular basis because I know his work is very demanding.

If your husband demonstrates his love for you and your family by getting up on a daily basis, going to work, and using the money he earns to pay for the household finances, then you should by all means let your husband know you appreciate him and always recognize his hard work.

Part 2 – I Still Had This Burning Question

Even though I didn't have an issue with Gordon's work ethic at all – and I was working as well – I still remember at some point wondering what God had in mind for my marriage. I genuinely wanted to know if this was it. Was this how He designed marriage to be? Never had I seen what a good marriage truly entailed. And even though I had never seen a truly good marriage (my parents had not been married), I still had a feeling that God must have had a phenomenal plan for my marriage. Though I didn't have any idea exactly what that plan was, I still wanted to know. And as I stood there, I thought, *God, is this the plan you have for me? Do You want me as the wife to be a just-there-and-going-along-with-the-flow kind of person?* I had these questions floating around in my mind because I thought marriage would be different. I had dreams we would talk to each other about anything and everything, enjoy being together, and be each other's best friend.

I Thought Things Would be Perfect

When I started falling for Gordon, we had gone on our second date to the Redondo Beach Pier. We played video games at the arcade and ended up walking along the beach holding hands while Gordon shared his heart with me. That was how I wanted it to be every day. Our life together would be just like that second date – perfect forever.

But things changed from that fairytale beginning, especially after we had Celeste, our first daughter. Our lines of communication began to be less open. At times, it seemed like Gordon would rather talk to anyone else but me. He would have conversations with family members and our children as they grew older, but when I would say we needed to converse more, he'd always reply, "What do you want to talk about?" That was frustrating because I just meant we weren't talking enough to each other, and I was growing weary of always needing to be the one to start a conversation. I knew silence wasn't what I wanted. What had happened from the time when we first walked and talked along the beach? Life happened, that's what happened! And just maybe we had begun to let things slip.

Remember back when you first started falling for your husband. Jot down a few highlights from that day or night. Where were you? What was it about him that made you start feeling there was something special about him? If it's been a really long time, dig out a picture that was taken of you two when you first met or when you were still all giggly and so in love. Now that you've been married for a while, how has your relationship changed?

_____

_____

_____

_____

_____

_____

_____

_____

Maybe you have asked similar questions as I did about your marriage? Perhaps you've been wondering whether your marriage is going the way God meant it to be. Like me, maybe you have wondered what God had in store for you as a wife? With something as important as our marriages, I thought we should go to the source, God's Word, and figure out exactly what God had in mind when He created marriage. What was God's original plan and design for us? We will find our answers by going back to when God first created marriage – when He created Eve, Adam's wife. However, before we review God's overall plan for marriage, let's take a look at how God expects us wives to conduct ourselves when dealing with our husbands.

Part 3 –Wives Should Submit

I've already talked about the husband's role as provider and how God has commanded them to love their wives as Christ loved the Church and laid His life down for it. This is now the other side of that coin: Wives have a role to play in God's design for marriage also.

"Wives, submit to your own husbands, as to the Lord. For the husband is head of the wife, as also Christ is head of the church; and He is the Savior of the body. Therefore, just as the church is subject to Christ, so let the wives be to their own husbands in everything." (Ephesians 5:22-24)

I know. I had to go and type that terrible six-letter word we wives do not like to hear: submit. But that is why I gave you the verses that pertain to your husband first. I wanted you to see the kind of standard to which God is holding him. His standard for your husband is Christ-like leadership. And God tells us to "submit to [our] own husbands, as to the Lord." What God is saying here is submit to your husbands like you submit to Him.

You see, God does not force us to submit to Him;

submission is a choice we make. The Greek word "hupotasso" is where we can derive the original meaning of what is being portrayed here. Hupo, means "under," and tasso, means "to order." Putting the two meanings together, hupotasso means "to order under." The *Lexical Aids to the New Testament* states the word hupotasso means "To place in an orderly fashion under something." It makes sense that in a marriage, there needs to be some order. It's like with your favorite team or movie, there can't be two head coaches or two directors. Someone has to be the leader – the main one calling the shots.

If your husband loves you just as Christ loved the church and gave himself for her, then you should not have to be coerced into submission to his leadership. Submitting should feel more like a natural response to that kind of love. I like how *The Message* translation says it:

"Wives, understand and support your husbands in ways that show your support for Christ. The husband provides leadership to his wife the way Christ does to his church, not by domineering but by cherishing. So just as the church submits to Christ as he exercises such leadership, wives should likewise submit to their husbands." (Ephesians 5: 22 – 24 MSG)

I also really like what Pastor Charles Stanley had to say about submission:

"Depending on the circumstance, submission can be positive or negative. When it's imposed, relationships are corrupted, and people are wounded. (That's one reason we condemn slavery and human trafficking.) But when submission is voluntary, it becomes a beautiful expression of love – which is what characterizes followers of Jesus. Consider the relationship between God and His Son. The Father didn't demand Jesus' death for our sins – Jesus chose to lay down His life (John 10: 17 –18). This willing and active participation in God's plan bears no resemblance to the forced obedience we typically imagine when we think of submission. The same is true for us: The exhortation to yield to one another (Eph. 5: 21) is an invitation to exercise the freedom God has given us. And in that way, we experience fellowship with Him. What kind of relationships would we have if loved ones forced us to serve them, or if God forced us to worship? Thankfully, He's given us a choice, and each time we yield to Him –- or to family and friends as appropriate --- we taste true freedom." (In Touch Daily Readings for Devoted Living, October 10, 2021)

What this says to me is when I submit to my husband's leadership regarding a decision he is discussing with me, I don't have to try to push my opinion or way of doing things on him. I can give my opinion or suggestion, and then I can exercise my freedom to give him my blessing (as appropriate as Pastor Stanley added) if it's something he really wants to do. If it's something you can live with, even if something goes wrong or a mistake is made, you can pray about it and just rest in the fact that God is pleased when you yield to your husband's way of handling a matter.

Also, we need to be careful about trying to weigh in on topics that men normally handle, like making repairs to the cars or repairs to the home, items at which he has more expertise than we do anyway (in most cases). And know that if things don't work out, he will have learned a lesson from it, especially if you don't fight him on it. Believe me, God has a way of teaching our husbands the lessons they need on His own. God really does not need our help.

Submission does not include any of the following:
1.   Being someone's door mat.
2.   Ceasing to have an identity of your own with no individual goals and accomplishments.
3.   Being timid or afraid of your husband and going along blindly with everything that your husband does or says.

Part 4 – God's Plan for Oneness in Your Marriage

The process God used to create Eve gives the next insight into God's plan for your marriage. Genesis chapter two says:

> "And the LORD God caused a deep sleep to fall upon Adam, and he slept: and He took one of his ribs, and closed up the flesh instead thereof, And the rib, which the LORD God had taken from man, made He a woman, and brought her unto the man. And Adam said, "This is now bone of my bones, and flesh of my flesh: she shall be called Woman, because she was taken out of Man." Therefore, shall a man leave his father and his mother and shall cleave

unto his wife: and they shall be one flesh."
(Genesis 2:21 – 24, KJV)

The last verse in this passage, verse 24, states
God's plan for you and your husband: That the two of
you would be one flesh. Verse 24 starts out with the
word "therefore." That means being one flesh is a direct
result of what is previously stated – namely verses 22
and 23. Adam has just stated how the woman is "bone
of his bones, and flesh of his flesh." She was literally
taken out of his side.

Stop and think about that. God did not choose to
make Adam's wife in the same way He had created
Adam. Adam was created from the dust of the earth
(Gen. 2:7). Eve was created from Adam's own flesh
and bones. Adam and Eve were truly "one flesh!" There
is a connection you have with your husband that no one
else can come close to, not even his parents. Adam
called his wife woman because she was taken out of
man.

The last verse of that passage says, "Therefore…
a man should leave his parents and cleave to his wife,
and they will be one flesh." One of my most heartfelt
desires for Gordon and me when we first got married
was that we would be one. I bought a plaque that says,
"And the Two Shall Become One." That plaque still
hangs in our home. Somehow, I knew back then God's
plan for my marriage was that we would be like one
flesh.

Here are eight roadblocks to a couple really being
able to achieve God's plan of being one:

1. No Room for Big Secrets

Husbands and wives must not keep secrets from
one another such as the following:

- Children they fathered, gave birth to, or gave up for adoption
  - Previous marriages
  - Relationships with exes
  - Current or former drug addictions
  - Incarcerations
  - Criminal record
  - Bad credit and/or excessive debts
  - Etc.

Secrets definitely do not help you to become one with your spouse. This does not mean, however, that you should go searching into your husband's personal belongings looking for some sort of secret. As the old saying goes: If you're looking for something wrong, you will most likely find something. Be open and honest with each other.

If a husband's or wife's family knows about secrets, their knowledge can lead to a situation in which the unknowing spouse may feel betrayed and left out of matters to which they were not privy. Secrets divide and create mistrust. Family members who are aware of any kind of deception should strongly encourage the one who has kept the secret, to tell the spouse as soon as possible.

I have experienced this myself. Gordon had a son when we got married; however, he did not tell me about him. Gordon told me when I was pregnant with our youngest daughter, Allison. He was very apologetic before he told me. Still finding this out was very difficult for me mainly because I had so many questions due to being left out of the loop. I was hurt because it felt like everyone else knew but me. For this reason, I thought about getting a divorce. I thank God for my mother-in-law and my dad who advised me to stay in my marriage and not let things go. Later on, God also showed me that it was His will that I would uphold my marriage vows, even though it hurt to do so. Thus, the revealing of Psalm 15 and the basis for the book that you are reading!

If you have experienced something similar, where secrets came out after your wedding day, you may still be feeling the sting of it all. I recommend you talk it over with someone who will give you some wisdom about your decision. And pray, of course. Depending on the seriousness of the situation, most likely you can forgive your husband and move forward with your marriage. Ask God to assist you with the process of forgiving your spouse, and any others involved, and move on. You only hurt yourself more by spending months, years, or even the rest of your life re-hashing the situation out in your mind.

I can tell you this: God knew about whatever the secret was and if it would end the marriage. If it was something serious, He may have tried to warn you about it before you tied the knot, but you did not listen or heed that warning. In fact, God may have somehow made you aware (maybe in a dream) that your husband was holding back some truth or event that had taken place. That's exactly what he did for me. God had already let me know in a dream – a few months earlier – that Gordon was keeping something from me. God is amazing and His wonders never cease!

I wasted a lot of time talking about this situation and being upset. Try not to be the woman who talks about a bad experience that happened 5, 10, 20, 30, or even 40 years later, and then speaks of it like it just happened last week! If you can live with it, forgive, move on, and live your life! In the end, I realized I needed to forgive my husband, especially since I needed Jesus to forgive me for my sins.

2. In Order to Cleave, You've Got to Leave

In Genesis 2, God is saying in a marriage, the husband will leave whoever nurtured and took care of him as a child and then stick close to his wife so he and his wife will become one flesh. How will a husband and wife be able to cleave to each other? And how will they achieve a state of oneness? The first way is exactly how it is described in this verse: The husband and wife will have to leave their mother and father.

It will be difficult to be one with your spouse if you are living in a parent's home, or if you or your husband haven't emotionally left your parents. You should not call mom and dad whenever there is a disagreement or a problem. Parents also should not be intertwined in your business or your household. You must move away from the original family that existed prior to the marriage. Family members should respect your new family, and work on giving this new organism room to grow and flourish on its own. If you notice anything unusual, or if your husband has a hard time separating emotionally from his family, pray and ask God to give you insight into the reason behind it and wisdom about what to do or what to say about it. It is good to set boundaries, early on as possible, that protect your peace and sense of self. That brings us to the next hinderance to couples being one.

3. Family Baggage

Each spouse has his or her own family background, and each one will bring along their own experience of family life into the marriage. Whether you were aware of this fact before you got married or not, the familial experiences that your mate has had will almost always have an impact on your marriage. Sometimes, you may not understand exactly what drives your husband to relate to his family, you, or your children the way that he does. This is true for yourself as well. Each family has its own individual culture, practices, and sometimes baggage that are unique from other families.

If you have a hard time cutting the apron strings between you and your mother or your father, get over it. You have got to leave the apron and those apron strings behind you. Honor your husband and give him his due props as the man in charge of your family. Look up to him and speak highly of him in front of your children and family members. And do not let anyone speak otherwise in your presence. It's important that your husband conducts himself in a way that is respectful to you as well, in front of and with his family. If your husband seems to need help being the leader, pray daily and fervently for him, God will definitely answer you!

Another part of this family baggage has to do with how each of your parents' roles were set up as husband and wife. In my case, there wasn't a husband in the home, so this required me to partially unlearn how I grew up.

4. Men Should Listen

Husbands should not make decisions independently of their wives or continue to carry on like they did when they were still single. Men should listen to their wives and take under consideration what they have to say. If you are married, and then you tell your spouse that she doesn't have a voice when it comes to important decisions, you are being insensitive. Your spouse will feel overlooked and made to feel that she doesn't matter in the relationship. This is absolutely not how God meant marriage to be. Operating in this manner will destroy any feelings of "oneness" in your marriage. You may be well-intentioned and feel things are just getting done faster by making decisions on your own, but that is not what God had in mind when He said for us to be one flesh.

5. Remember Eve's Mistake

Women should not try to control the household, finances, or their husband. Just think about Eve's mistake in listening to the cunning craftiness of the serpent. (Read Genesis 3: 1–13.) Eve's bad decision caused mankind to be under a curse. But thank God, Jesus came to save us from that curse! (See 1 Corinthians 15:22.) If it had not been for Jesus, we wives would have it pretty bad – our husbands would be ruling over us and it would be all Eve's fault! (See Genesis 3: 16.) But honestly, we can't ignore the fact that Adam just went along with Eve and didn't speak up when she picked and ate the forbidden fruit. That gets back to men needing to be the leaders in the household. And wives, we must encourage our husbands to be that leader.

6. Money Matters

Wives, money matters cause more problems in marriage than lots of other issues. Many husbands equate managing the money with their position as the leader in the home. Taking money out of your bank accounts or making charges on credit cards without your husband's knowledge can easily upset the balance of cooperation in your home. Even if a wife makes more money and is better at keeping the finances straight and paying the bills, the husband—as the leader in the home—needs to be allowed to be the final word on financial matters. (A husband who is weak in the areas of financial responsibility and knowledge is wise to take financial advice from his wife.) A wife who lends her financial strength to her husband builds him as a husband, supports him as her leader, and respects his manhood.

If your husband makes more money than you make, he should not lord that over you and you should respect their household budget. If you are working outside of the home or perhaps you're operating an in-home business, once you pitch in your agreed-upon amount for the household, the rest is yours to enjoy and use for yourself. I am a firm believer that when you have earned income of your own, you should be able to buy yourself something nice from time-to-time. This is a reward to yourself. It might be a trip to the hair or nail salon, buying a nice outfit for church or work, or all of the above. Again, what either of you spend on yourselves should not take away from bills getting paid. Wives and husbands alike should not charge up debt for unnecessary items or reasons.

Issues involving spouses spending money that the other one does not agree with, or has no knowledge of, is one of the biggest hinderances to couples truly being one, happy, and having peace within your marriage. Your husband should not be conducting financial transactions with friends, business associates, or family members, without sitting down and discussing those transactions in detail with you. And of course, if he shouldn't be doing this, then neither should you. So, it is important that you and your husband be united as one team when handling business matters and finances. That team should consist of just the two of you, not three, four, or more individuals.

7. T.H.I.N.K. Before You Speak Your Peace

Sometimes, it is what and how we say things that can form a divide between us and our mates thereby affecting the oneness shared. We do need to be honest and as forthright as possible with each other. I must confess I have been the poster child for oftentimes not going about speaking my peace to Gordon in the most tactful way. It's not that I was being disrespectful towards him, it's just that I didn't phrase my sentences in the correct way. Like the young people say, "You have got to come correct." Instead, I have often found myself just saying something to him without giving it a second thought, and thereby putting my whole foot in my mouth. And next, wondering why he became so upset, or just shut down completely. Something I heard my pastor, Bayless Conley, teach is, "T.H.I.N.K. before you speak."

Is it True?

Is it Helpful?

Is it Inspiring?

Is it Necessary?

Is it Kind? (Accessed February 7, 2022, www.jdaniellowe.com/healthymarriages, "Quotes of Marriage," n.d.)

So, it would be wise if we wives (and our husbands) would take a few minutes to go through the above acronym and think exactly how we want to present what we have to say prior to saying it. You should also pray, asking God to show you the right time and the right words to speak – especially if you will be delving into a topic your husband doesn't necessarily want to hear. I cannot emphasize enough the importance of praying, thinking, and waiting for the proper timing before you speak.

Here is a recommended order for speaking your peace about something your husband is or is not doing. Give him what he needs, and if he's not giving you what you need, then tell him. Oftentimes, we wives want to point the finger, but in fact we aren't doing our part either.

Also, try to always start your conversations with an affirmation such as, "I really appreciated it today when you _____." (For more conversation starters see www.jdaniellowe.com/healthymarriages, accessed on February 7, 2022.) Always do your best to keep your tone upbeat and respectful. Equally important is that you speak up about necessary issues as early on in the relationship as possible. It is not healthy to just let things fester and not say anything about what is bothering you.

Prayerfully pick your battles and remember that sometimes the best way to deal with issues in your marriage is to use the "shut up and pray" technique. You know the old saying, "Silence is golden"? When you get silent and just go into your prayer closet, well, *that* ladies is an effective strategy because prayer is a weapon. (And the weapon is not against your husband, it's against the enemy of our marriages – the devil.) And, IF you do speak up and your husband doesn't do the right thing, then just put him in the hands of the Lord. Remember, your husband will have to answer to

God (just as we ALL will one day) and God says vengeance is His; He will repay!

8. A Lack of Sex or Lovemaking

A lack of physically joining together, therefore becoming one flesh physically, as well as spiritually is a big hinderance to you and your spouse being one. This is when your marriage is missing sex, or more appropriately lovemaking, your relationship will suffer. I will go over the difference between sex and making love in Chapter 4.

There are eight important areas I have written about so far that can help or hinder oneness in your marriage. Which of the above areas do you feel you may need to prayerfully address within your marriage?

_____
_____
_____
_____
_____
_____
_____
_____
_____

Sticking Together Like Glue

While lovemaking and sexual encounters between a husband and wife are vital and extremely important to oneness in marriage, to cleave to someone involves much more than just having a sexual union. After all, this is why so many sexual affairs do not last and end up with the couple either moving on to another affair or trying to go back to their spouse. There is an element missing when the relationship is not founded within the confines of God's will and when the relationship is purely sexual. That missing element is the glue of God's power to hold the marriage together.

The original Hebrew word for "cleave" is "dabaq" (daw-bak), meaning "to cling or adhere, cleave, follow close, be joined together... stick closer." The following explanation of the meaning of dabaq is found in the book *Prayers That Avail Much for Mothers,* Word Ministries, Inc.:

"...to cling to, *to adhere to firmly as if with glue.*" It also is used in a loving and devoted way to mean "to be attached to someone or something by the heart strings," Dabaq also can be defined as "clinging to someone in affection or loyalty." ...It is the same word as used in Genesis to describe what happens in marriage: A man shall leave his father and mother and shall "cleave" to his wife. (Gen.2:24) In this verse the word **cleave** is dabaq. It expresses the concept of "staying real close to someone." [1]

Inviting God in the Midst of Your Marriage Will Help You "Stick"

One of the definitions of dabaq mentions sticking together as if with glue. What is the glue that might help the couple stick? Of course, the answer is God, Himself! God is in fact the glue and is necessary to be a central part of the union. In Ecclesiastes, Solomon, the son of King David, who was said to have been one of the wisest men in the Bible, wrote:

"Two people are better off than one, for they can help each other succeed. If one person falls, the other can reach out and help. But someone who falls alone is in real trouble. Likewise, two people lying close together can keep each other warm. But how can one be warm alone? A person standing alone can be attacked and defeated, but two can stand back-to-back and conquer. Three are even better, for a triple-braided cord is not easily broken." (Ecclesiastes 4:9-12, NLT)

A Threefold Cord

That third strand in the triple-braided cord is talking about God, our Creator, the only One (other than His Son, Jesus, and the Holy Spirit) Who is able to keep all things together. When we entrust our lives to God, and receive His Son Jesus Christ as our Savior, we will love Jesus and obey His teachings. And as a result, Jesus and God come to abide in us. (John 14:21-23) Jesus said if we stay vitally united to Him, He will abide in us, and we will be able to bear much fruit. He also says that outside of staying connected to Him, we will be unfruitful, just as a branch cannot grow fruit away from the vine. (John 15:4)

When we humble ourselves and invite Jesus to be the Lord of our lives, we die to the carnal way of living and invite Him to be at the center of everything we do. That is what surrendering means. If we ask God to assist us in our union with our mates, He comes and abides in the midst of that too. That's when we will have that threefold cord taking place within our marriage. So, in order to truly be one with each other, we need to first become one with the Lord. That is exactly how he will be able to come into the midst of our marriage.

Take some time now to reflect on what God wanted to happen in marriage when He created it. What are some of the ways that will help us to truly be one with our mates? Answer this question: Have you brought God into every aspect of your life, including every part of your marriage? Take a moment and write in your own words a few of the key components that will help oneness truly take place in your marriage.

_____

_____

_____

_____

_____

_____

_____

_____

_____

_____

Chapter Four

Your Needs and His Needs: They Both Matter!

⁓

I had convinced myself that something was wrong with this life we call marriage. Sometimes while out with Gordon, I would notice other couples and observe their behavior. I began to think to myself, *See, that couple isn't married because the guy is still acting romantic towards the lady he's with!* and *Look, I can tell that couple has been married for a few years because they're just sitting there on their phones, not even saying a word to each other.* I started to blame the husbands of the non-affectionate couples and would be thinking, *He's already made his catch now, so there's no need for him to act like he's pursuing her anymore.*

Then I started noticing this phenomenon in my own marriage, so on one of our outings together, I mentioned it to Gordon. I pointed out that it didn't seem fair that husbands changed after they got married. He said, "What makes you think that *relationships* don't change after several years?" He went on to say in a sense that our relationship had changed because of conflict. He also seemed to be inferring that I had changed too.

After being passive about things I didn't like in our marriage for several years, I had started speaking up about them to my husband. It felt good and like I was getting some of my power back in the marriage. I was finally letting it be known that there were things I didn't care for. But what I ended up figuring out was that if I truly wanted my husband to treat me like he did before we got married, I would need to get back in touch with the girlfriend I had been to him. At the same time, Gordon needed to remember how he treated me on that wonderful evening at Redondo Beach that started creating the magnet that drew my heart closer to his. We both needed to revisit what the other one needed, to ensure we continued to experience a satisfied and happy marriage.

Part 1 -- Wives Need Affection (Not Just Sex)

Wives need romance and encouraging words. Affection or romance, and kindness are some of the key ingredients that assure couples have truly become one in marriage. A husband's true affection involves communicating with his actions that he loves, adores, and appreciates his wife above all other women. A husband's positive actions in this area can lead to feelings of security in his wife. Conversely, when a husband neglects to show these actions, his wife is likely to feel insecure.

1 Corinthians, chapter seven, says:

"Let the husband render to his wife the affection due her, and likewise also the wife to her husband. The wife does not have authority over her own body, but the husband *does.* And likewise the husband does not have authority over his own body, but the wife *does.* Do not deprive one another except with consent for a time, that you may give yourselves to fasting and prayer; and come together again so that Satan does not tempt you because of your lack of self-control." (1 Corinthians 7:3-5)

Notice that verse 3 does not say for the husband to render the "sex" that is due to his wife. It clearly states that he is to give her the "affection" that is due to her. Some translations just speak about the "conjugal rights" of the wife and the "duty of a husband" in this verse. But the Amplified translation mentions the true meaning of the original Greek word "eunoia" used for affection which means "to favor, benevolence, good will." Benevolence also means "kindness." I Corinthians 7:3 in the Amplified Bible reads as follows:

"The husband must fulfill his [marital] duty to his wife [*with good will and kindness*], and likewise the wife to her husband." (Emphasis added.)

What has happened when husbands are lacking in kindness, patience, and attention for their wives? Husbands are sometimes guilty of spending a lot of time seemingly just staring at the television screen. I mean, it's like they're afraid that they'll miss a pin being dropped during a commercial! Or they may want to hang out with their friends too much. These activities can all contribute to a lack of affection and true oneness in the marriage. A man should also take time and care to get his wife into the right mood for when the time comes for making love. We are not aroused simply by the sight of our mate's naked bodies, like men are excited by the sight of ours. Williard F. Harley, author of the well-known book *His Needs, Her Needs*, wrote the following on this topic:

"A lot of husbands do remember the passionate encounters of their courting days and want to know, "Why doesn't she get turned on the way she used to, now that we're married?" I patiently explain that she isn't getting turned on now because he isn't treating her as he did then. Does he think getting married suddenly eliminates the woman's need for affection? A man should work as carefully and patiently at showing affection in his marriage as he did when he and his wife dated. Only after a woman has received affection for a time will she become one with a man physically, but affection *must* come before sex." [1]

Let's say that your husband only thinks he needs to be affectionate when he wants sex. Well, that most likely makes you feel not in the mood a lot of times. Even if you actually want to make love with your husband, your body isn't ready because your mind hasn't been stimulated. Even with some really good foreplay, you can still be left feeling disconnected emotionally from your husband. Wives need their husbands to be loving, romantic, and sensitive every day, and it needs to start much earlier in the day than right before sex or love making.

Part 2 -- Men Want Sex, Women Want to Make Love

Sometimes I use the word "sex" and other times the phrase "making love." Why is that? Making love is what most wives want, but oftentimes, husbands may just be satisfied with having sex. Making love is a direct result of your husband rendering the affection (gentleness, kindness, and attention) that is due to you, along with spending quality time with you. This is because women experience arousal primarily through their brains. For example, I'm sure you have heard that old adage "Sex begins in the kitchen." Perhaps the saying should be "Making love begins in the kitchen." Making love has little to do with the food being prepared or eaten in the kitchen. Sex is elevated to love making depending on the interaction that is or is not taking place earlier in the day, such as when the wife is making a meal or the husband is just sitting eating the meal.

Your husband will also experience more sexual fulfillment because you will give yourself more freely to him and he will notice the difference. I feel this is another very important way a married couple can achieve the oneness spoken of in Genesis chapter 2. When a wife gives all of herself without holding back any part of her emotions because she feels truly loved, understood, and appreciated – that is when true lovemaking takes place and therefore oneness takes place within the marriage.

But Do We Both Know How to Be Affectionate?

What happens if your husband doesn't know how to be affectionate outside of the advances leading up to sex? Heck, even as a wife, we may need a little help in this department as well. My mom used to always tell me that she wasn't raised in a family that hugged and kissed a lot. That was her way of saying she didn't know how to show affection that well. Sometimes, I ask myself if I was affectionate enough with my own children. And what about with my husband? This is when we may need to ask for some help from others.

Here are some suggested ways you and your husband can express affection for one another. You and your husband can read these suggested actions together or you could ask him if he minds you reading them to him.

Things you both can do to show each other affection:

1.   Kiss each other goodbye when you leave and when you return from work.

2.   Send a flirty text and respond to each other briefly during the workday.

3.   Make a meal, or a healthy salad for dinner. Or order some healthy takeout.

4.   Make the other one breakfast and serve it, even if it's breakfast in bed.

5.   Say something complimentary about each other to someone else so your spouse can hear it.

6.   Defend each other; never let anyone say anything negative about the other one.

7.   Desire to be intimate only with each other.

8.   Tell each other that you're each other's best friend. No one else of the opposite

sex should be your best friend other than your spouse.

9.   Laugh together.

10.   Listen to each other's favorite musicians or artists and sing together or to each other.

11.   Make eye contact when you are talking.

12.   Put down your phones and pay attention; listen to each other.

13.   Hold hands or put your arm around each other.

14.   Be there for each other when one is sick. Go to the drugstore, go to the hospital, make meals, etc.

15.   Plan a special night out together. Have day or weekend getaways.

16.   Cook a meal together.

Things you can do to show your husband affection:

1.   Give him hugs just because.

2.   Kiss him passionately.

3.   Initiate lovemaking and show him you desire him physically.

4.   Let him know you're his biggest fan by your words and actions.

5.   Leave him thoughtful notes on his pillow, or in his shoulder bag, backpack, or workout bag, to show your love and appreciation. Try *Loving Reminders for Couples: 60 Affectionate Notes & Stickers for Those Close to your Heart,* by Franklin Covey, or make handwritten ones.

6.   Tell him how handsome he looks before he leaves for work in the mornings, and when he's going out with or without you at other times.

7.   Make him breakfast or a healthy smoothie in the mornings, or the night before.

8.   Be energetic and enthusiastic about making love with him.

Things your husband can do to show you affection:

1.   Make you a cup of coffee or tea.

2.   Give you a wink or a pat on the butt when passing by you.

3.   Tell you that you look cute before you leave for work, on the way to church, when on a date, or at any other time.

4.   Give you a kiss on the cheek just because.

5.   Let you know he's leaving the house and where he's going, and when he's on his way home.

6.   Be protective of you and look out for your safety.

7.   Ask you to come sit by him when he's watching T.V.

8.   Tell you he needs you and loves you without expecting sex in return.

9.   Tell you how much he loves you before, during, or after you've made love.

10.   Take time to check on you and ask you how you're feeling.

11.   Bring you flowers just because.

12.   Wash or fix your car.

13.   Pick up something you need from the market.

14.   Open the car door for you.

15.   Walk beside you and talk or listen while walking.

16.   Hold the door for you.

You may have noticed that the husbands' list is longer than the wives' list. But remember, wives' number one need is affection, so this makes sense. These lists are not complete. Nor is every action on these lists something you or your hubby might find affectionate. You two can discuss which ones you would like the other one to do along with the loving actions you are already doing.

Pray about your husband being more attentive and affectionate towards you – and you towards him. There is a very good prayer in the book *The Power of a Praying Wife* by Stormie Omartian. The "Affection" prayer in her book is highly effective if you pray it with faith. I have prayed this prayer and seen God answer it almost immediately. We need to make it a habit of regularly praying about ways we can show each other affection. Whenever things begin feeling a little bit dry between the two of you, go back to that prayer, and say it out loud. Or even better, don't wait until it's a problem.

A Little Creativity Never Hurts

In addition to doing some of the suggested actions above and praying, we wives must remember to use our creativity and find different ways to express affection for our husbands as well. According to the text in 1 Corinthians above, affection should be rendered to each other, so you cannot sit back and simply expect your husband to show affection while you are not showing much yourself. Do little things to spice up your marriage. Be thoughtful and kind to your husband as well. As the old saying goes, "You get a lot more bees with honey, than you do with vinegar."

The next Friday or Saturday evening that you have the house all to yourself (or you can plan to have someone keep the kids), dress up in a sexy negligée and put on some sexy heels. Take a relaxing bath before he arrives home and use some body crème that smells delicious. Greet him with a smile and a refreshing drink – you can make him a cocktail if he enjoys one every now and then – as well as a big hug and a kiss. Get creative and have fun with your hubby. You can play some nice romantic music and light candles if you two enjoy that sort of thing. Remember to act more like a girlfriend than a wife sometimes! Loosen up, dance to the music, have a little fun! You can perform a nice alluring dance for him if you want or dance together. Don't forget to have something for him to eat as well. You can just have something light to eat and perhaps the two of you can get away for a quick bite or dinner later.

Plan For a Better Outcome

As I mentioned in the beginning of this chapter, I had started noticing that I wasn't getting the affection that I wanted in my marriage. It's not like Gordon wasn't ever being affectionate, because he was. It just wasn't happening with the consistency I would have liked. But also, when I really began to reflect on how I would approach my husband with an issue or concern that I had in the marriage, I realized that I didn't have a plan. I wasn't taking into consideration the best time to approach my husband. Did I want to maybe prepare his favorite meal or at least make sure he was fed beforehand? When was the last time we had made love (or just had sex whatever the case may be)?

Part 3 -- Husbands Need Honor and Sex

I try to give my husband the respect he deserves. I am not saying I have always been perfect at this, but I have even asked Gordon occasionally if I am treating him respectfully, and he has said that I do. I think that is a good question to ask your husband from time-to-time. You can ask him to give you examples of when he has, or has not, felt honored by you. When I've asked him this question, Gordon has mentioned that my tone with him is sometimes incorrect. He also gets upset when I continue to bring up an issue that I've already discussed with him. As I stated in Chapter 3, we always want to keep our tone as upbeat and respectful as possible. I don't know about your husband, but mine isn't the type who takes well to things said in an improper way.

In the last verse of Ephesians chapter 5, the Bible summarizes how a husband and his wife should treat each other:

"However, each man among you [without exception] is to love his wife as his very own self [with behavior worthy of respect and esteem, always seeking the best for her with an attitude of lovingkindness], *and the wife [must see to it] that she respects and delights in her husband [that she notices him and prefers him and treats him with loving concern, treasuring him, honoring him, and holding him dear]*." (Ephesians 5:33 AMP, emphasis added)

As I was writing this chapter, I found some notes I had taken in church on this topic. I am not sure when or which church I was attending at the time, but I wrote:

"God commands the woman to honor and respect her husband. Be careful of the way you talk to your husband. Because the wife is the helpmate, she is always trying to "help" her husband. It's more helpful and easier to make "suggestions" to your husband. Don't talk *at him*... because he hears his mother when you do that. *Don't talk down to him*, but you do have to give some suggestions. God made the woman to bring glory to the man (or to add a benefit to him). So, if you have something to tell him that may embarrass him, wait until you get home! (Or take him aside.)

When a man opens up to share intimately, don't tell his business. When you don't trust each other, you're open to adultery. If you have told his secrets in the past, ask him to forgive you. If you're talking negatively about your spouse, cease from doing that. Build your spouse up properly and they'll never be looking to others for approval.
Does your spouse know that you're their number one fan? Does your spouse know that you would do anything for them?" (Speaker unknown)

A good way to let your husband know how much

you respect, honor, and love him is to do what he asks you to do. This has been something I have struggled with in the past. But honestly, at this moment, I cannot think of one time I have regretted doing (or yes, submitting to) what Gordon told me to do.

But I do remember a few times, early in our marriage, when I did not follow Gordon's wise advice, with not-so-favorable outcomes. Gordon and I had just moved in to our new townhome in Compton, California, so I went to see about purchasing a washer and dryer, and later needed to wash clothes. Gordon told me not to go to a laundromat in Compton. Not realizing that he must have had a good reason for telling me this, I went to one in Compton anyway.

While I was there washing our clothes, a young woman came walking through the laundromat waving a gun! This caused all of us who were there in the laundromat to immediately hit the floor! Thankfully, no one was injured or robbed, and I learned it pays to listen to the wisdom of my husband.

Conversely, wives are not under obligation to obey husbands who ask or demand that they do something dishonorable, potentially dangerous, or unwise. An example of this is found in Queen Vashti, in the book of Esther, chapter one. Queen Vashti refused to come when her husband – King Xerxes – commanded her to appear before a group of men who had been drinking and partying for a full week! He wanted her to come wearing her royal crown, and some Jewish accounts say he wanted her to come wearing *only* her crown. Even though Vashti could have been put to death for disobeying her husband's command, she chose to honor her modesty, and her safety instead.

Has your husband ever told you to do something, and you did not do it? Take a moment to think about that time. Did it turn out great, good, okay, or awful? What are some ways that you honor, or show respect, to your husband?

_____

_____

_____

_____

_____

_____

Give Your Husband What the Head Physician Ordered

Have you ever noticed that your husband is in a much better mood after you have given him some medicine? And I don't mean the kind of medicine that comes from a doctor's prescription. I mean the kind of medicine that only *you* can give him. This medicine has been prescribed by Almighty God Himself, and the order never expires! You and I want our husbands to be more affectionate, but are we being mindful to give them what they need?

Sexual fulfillment is extremely important to married men. Sex plays a deeper, more important role than you may know. First Corinthians 7:4, discussed earlier, begins with the command that the wife should not have authority over her own body, but the husband does. Therefore, we wives are not to unjustifiably withhold the act of making love from our husbands. And your husband is not to deny you the benefit of free access to his body. The only exception being during brief times of fasting and prayer. Also, if one is not feeling well, the other should be understanding. However, wives, we should not have a week-long (or a month-long) headache!

You may have noticed that I used the phrase "wives are not to *unjustifiably* withhold the act of making love...". The only justifiable time to withhold sex from our husbands – other than the two instances mentioned above – is if he has been unfaithful (committed adultery). I do also believe that if your husband has been incredibly unkind to you to the point of physical or emotional abuse, then that would also be a justifiable time as well, and it's best to get as far away from him as possible for your own safety.

How Often Should You Administer the Medication?

You may be wondering how often you should be having sex with your husband? I cannot tell you exactly because you should know your husband's physical stamina and what he can handle. But I suggest that you should be having sex or making love with your husband at least once per week. If you don't know how often your husband would prefer to come together sexually with you, then there is absolutely nothing wrong with you asking him. Your husband may want to have sex twice a week, or every other day, or even every day. If that is the case, then you may need to get creative and just try your best to meet his needs. There is nothing wrong with manipulating him with your hands on some occasions, but I don't suggest that you use that technique all of the time just because you don't want to make love.

Make a concerted effort to meet your husband's needs sexually. If you are tired, or don't feel good about your body, you can ask your husband to give you a few minutes. Take a relaxing bath or shower. You can ask him to give you a relaxing massage with oil or lotion, rub your feet for you, brush or comb your hair. Any one of these will help to relax you and make you more in the mood. Also, you can put on a sheer lingerie robe over your negligee if you are a little self-conscious about your body. Believe me, your husband is not going to be scrutinizing your body at this point; he just wants to be ravished with your love!

Can the "Marriage Bed" Be Defiled?

I want to discuss things that should not be done in the marriage bed. Most Christians are familiar with the verse in the Bible which states that the marriage bed is undefiled, and their conclusion, based on their understanding is that a married couple may do whatever they want sexually. This is not true. First, let's read the verse, from Hebrews, chapter 13, in the New King James Version:

"Marriage *is* honorable among all, and the bed undefiled; but fornicators and adulterers God will judge." (Hebrews 13: 4)

Here is the same verse in another translation:

"Marriage should be honored by all, and the marriage bed kept pure, for God will judge the adulterer and all the sexually immoral. (NIV)

It is clear, from reading these two versions of the text, that marriage should be respected by everyone, and the "marriage bed" is to be kept undefiled. The Greek word for undefiled is "amiantos", which means unpolluted.

But what has the potential of polluting your marriage bed? The second translation seems to answer this question: Keep the marriage bed pure, because God is going to judge adulterers and those who have sexual vices. So obviously, married folks are to steer clear of having sexual relationships with anyone they are not married to. But, also, we are to eliminate any sexual vices that we may have such as:

1. Pornography - the Greek word for "fornication" (sexual immorality in some translations) is "porneia". Jesus said that looking at a woman and lusting for her is tantamount to adultery:

"But I say to you that whoever looks at a woman to lust for her has already committed adultery with her in his heart." (Matthew 5:28)

2. Lustful thoughts about someone other than your spouse. Passionate thoughts should be reserved for your spouse. Based on the following scriptures, it would be wrong for a man (or a woman) to think about someone else (even their celebrity crush) while they are having sex with their husband, or any other time:

"Do not lust in your heart after her beauty or let her captivate you with her eyes." (Proverbs 6:25 NIV)

But if they cannot control themselves, they should marry, for it is better to marry than to burn with passion. (I Corinthians 7:9 NIV)

According to an article on neverthirsty.org:

"The same is true for women since some women read magazines containing naked photos of men and some visit male strip clubs. They must not engage in such activity. Women can sin when they lust after or daydream about a man because of his character such as his kindness, mercy, grace, wealth, and reputation. Sin occurs when a male or female lusts after or daydreams about anyone to whom they are not married. But it is not a sin for a husband to dream about or sexually desire his wife or for a wife to do the same toward her husband. Again, God designed husbands and wives to respond that way within marriage. God commands husbands and wives to satisfy each other's sexual passions." ("When does sexual passion become the sin of lust?", www.neverthirsty.org, n.d.)

Don't Take Each Other For Granted

Neither the husband nor the wife should be guilty of taking the other one for granted! When they do so, Satan is prepared to come in and do his sly and cunning work to disturb and possibly break the marriage apart. Therefore, 1 Corinthians chapter 7, verse 5 quite clearly states the husband and wife are not to withhold or deprive one another of marital sex or lovemaking. Why? Simply because if this occurs, the couple's needs end up going unmet, and someone—if not both spouses—may begin to look to other individuals or situations to meet those unmet needs. You may be tempted to begin welcoming the attention and affectionate advances of a coworker or family friend. Your husband could begin to consider other ways to have his need for sexual satisfaction met be it from another person of the opposite sex, pornography, or frequent masturbation. Wives also find these same outlets. This is *not* what God has in mind for your marriage!

So, you see, there is no need for your husband to be affectionate towards you if you are going to be stingy in the love-making department. Your husband can't continue bringing you flowers or calling you during the day to whisper sweet nothings in your ear, or greeting you with a hug or a kiss, or telling you how much he loves and adores you, if you're just going to roll

over and turn your back towards him when the two of you go to bed. Or worse yet, perhaps you decide not to even go to bed when your husband does. At some point, his attention and kindness towards you needs to be rewarded. When it is not, this creates a problem in your marriage.

Also, your husband wants you to initiate sex with him sometimes. It lets him know that you desire him and want him physically. Just think how you would feel if you were the one always having to ask for sex and your husband never did. If that is the case already, try asking your husband why he is not initiating sex. It could be that he is extremely stressed from work or business. Sometimes, you may need to just plan to get him away from it all. Pray and ask God to show you where and when you two can get away. Make some reservations: book a hotel room, prepare a romantic dinner, order room service, go somewhere fun that he would love. Then rock his world!

Stay True to Who God Says You Are

God is the only One who is able to supply our every need. So even though sometimes our husbands do things that can make us very frustrated, as true women of God, we cannot do things that are contrary to the integrity within us and who the Bible says we are. We have to run to our heavenly Father with all of our needs. We have to surrender ourselves to Him one hundred percent and give our husband and marriage over to Him, entrusting God to work on him *and* on us. And in the meantime, we have to live our best life which is to live in the will of God.

The key is to read the Word and pray daily, making sure we are being open and transparent with our heavenly Father. A great way to start your day is by using devotionals in which you are given scripture to read and then a life application to practice. *In Touch Ministries* (intouch.org) offers great daily devotions and I love them! God has really used this resource to speak exactly what I have needed when I have needed it. I also read my *Daily Devotional Bible* to try to get through the Bible in a year.

Part 4 – Wives Need Conversation, Husbands Need Companionship

Besides wives needing our husbands to show us kindness, affection, and appreciation, we also have a tremendous need for conversation. As I mentioned earlier, the way Gordon opened up and talked with me on our second date was critical to him winning my heart. Husbands should remember what they did to win their wives over and continue doing those things throughout the marriage. Of course, this also applies to wives as well. The Bible tells husbands not to be ignorant about the innate qualities that make up their wives. In fact, it indicates that understanding his wife is essential even for his prayers to be answered!

> "Likewise, husbands, live with your wives in an understanding way, showing honor to the woman as the weaker vessel, since they are heirs with you of the grace of life, so that your prayers may not be hindered." (1 Peter 3:7 ESV)

This verse is saying that if they want their prayers to be answered, husbands need to show honor to their wives and treat them delicately, understanding she is on equal standing with him as an heir in the sight of God.

Oftentimes, it appears that husbands forget, willfully abandon, or do not actually know how to verbalize their care and adoration for their wives. Instead, men can get so caught up in pressures at work, television, sports, hobbies, their cellphones, friends and family members, or pressures at work that they forget to turn and fix their eyes on the One who is walking by their side daily in life! Women beware because we can become guilty of the very same distractions!

We, as couples, need to put everything down periodically, turn off the television and the cellphones, and spend quality time with each other. We need to forget about all the mundane stuff that can become the subjects of our marriage and talk about the things that we need to share with the most special person in our lives, our spouse! For help with starting conversations with your husband, you can try using *88 Conversation Starters for Husbands & Wives* by Christian Art Gifts. Gordon and I have used them, and I highly recommend them.

I was praying one day, and God showed me a startling analogy. I was asking God to forgive me for not prioritizing my prayer time, and God allowed me to see that not wanting to spend time in prayer with Him was just like my husband not wanting to engage in conversation with me. Think about how we as Christians oftentimes become lazy about spending time regularly with God in fellowship and prayer. Does our failure to spend time with God mean that we don't love Him? No, I think it just represents our failure to understand how much more we would benefit from investing time in the relationship.

Sometimes, we take God for granted like we do our spouses. More specifically, husbands sometimes appear to take their wives for granted like we do to God. A husband may just want his wife to provide what he needs without spending the quality time with her that she needs. And let's not mention how we wives can be oh so guilty of taking our husbands for granted too! We want him to go to work every day and pay the bills, but sometimes we fail to truly look at that man with adoration and respect, seeing what he needs and wants. Do these behaviors mean one has fallen out of love with the other? Not always. In fact, if a man is still there with you and coming home every night, that's a sign he still is in love with you and wants to be in the relationship. Additionally, you would probably not be reading this book if you were not still in love with your husband.

We just need to remind ourselves often of why we got together in the first place. I really do think it is very well worth it to pull out those wedding photos periodically, dust them off, and spend some time looking at them. Also, look at the recording of your wedding ceremony. This is priceless!

Men Need Companionship from Their Wives

In the book *His Needs Her Needs* by Willard F. Harley, the author tells a true story about a couple. Prior to the couple marrying, the wife would often play tennis with her husband. This was the type of companionship the husband enjoyed, and consequently this was a major factor apparently in why he married his wife. After they got married, the wife no longer would agree to accompany her husband to play tennis. She apparently had only gone along with playing tennis to make a good initial impression on him and to win him over.

Consequently, the husband ended up finding another companion to play tennis with—another woman. Long story short, the man ended up leaving his wife for the new tennis companion. He felt betrayed by his wife that she had only pretended to be athletically inclined before they married. That had been very important to him because he wanted a companion to participate in his athletic endeavors.

This story was meant to illustrate how important it is that you spend time with your husband doing whatever he enjoys doing. I read recently how Joyce Meyers, well-known Christian women's conference speaker and author, said her husband was always asking her to play golf with him. She said she really didn't want to go, but she thought about all of the times he accompanied her to her conferences. So, she ended up going to watch him play golf, and it was a blessing for her seeing him doing something he enjoyed doing so much.

If conversation is a missing element in your marriage, you can possibly meet both your need for conversation and his need for companionship while participating in some activity he enjoys. Maybe your husband has a favorite sports team or a favorite television show. Join in and watch the games or television shows with him. Get into the games or shows and pay attention. Ask him a few quick questions (during the timeouts or the commercials) to get a better understanding from his expertise (not too many though). Listen attentively as he is talking to you and be genuinely interested. If you aren't interested, he is going to figure that out. Cuddle up or sit close to him while the game or show is on. I believe this approach is far better than you simply being in a stand-off with your husband: waiting for him to make a move in your direction and deciding you will not move in his direction until he approaches you.

If you begin talking about something he enjoys, then there's at least some conversation going on. Then, we need to get some regular prayer to our heavenly Father about the husband's need to communicate on a more intimate level. I cannot emphasize enough that prayer is of great necessity in a marriage. And really, we cannot forget this necessity. Prayer needs to be a regular component in your marriage. More about prayer in Chapter 7.

Part 5 – Kicking Out the Boredom Demon!

It took 6 years before Gordon and I were blessed to have our oldest daughter, Celeste. I had fertility issues and had to get treatment. Believe me, there was much prayer involved in the process. Then we had Allison almost exactly 3 years later! But I noticed that after Gordon and I had our first child, our marriage changed. You might say, "Duh, of course it changed! You now have a child in the family." But I mean that our *relationship* changed. There were so many other responsibilities now, and it became easy to get caught up in them. Gordon and I had always gone out of town on our anniversaries each year. But I noticed that we were letting that commitment to our marriage slip. So, I started making the arrangements for our annual anniversary getaways myself to help keep a sense of "us" in the marriage.

It is amazingly easy to become overwhelmed with the busyness of life, and with so many women working outside of the home, it is very easy for you to be exhausted at the end of the day. This is also true if you're working inside of the home raising children and trying to keep up the house. At the same time, men can become burned out from work situations and stresses. Then there's the kid's afterschool activities, homework, dinner, chores, etc. All of this can create an atmosphere in which days, weeks, or even months can go by without so much as even a kiss shared between the two of you.

Children should not come before your spouse. Don't rap up all your life in the kids. Kids grow up one day, leave home, and then you will be stuck with just each other again, but it won't be like it was when you were able to spend time together without the responsibility of children.

God meant for husbands and wives to enjoy each

other fully – that includes physically, romantically, and emotionally. Couples need to spend time alone. You're not going to have a great marriage by accident. Have dates. While it's wonderful when our husbands ask us out on a date, there's nothing wrong with you asking your husband. Having a regular date night is great. But remember, I'm talking about kicking out the boredom demon from your marriage. So even if you have a regular date night, do something spontaneous, fun, and exciting on your date night!

At the writing of this book, Gordon and I just celebrated our 31st anniversary, so I planned a trip to Pismo Beach. I made a dinner reservation for our first night there at a restaurant overlooking the ocean. Before we left, we shared part of our celebration with our kids by opening the gifts they bought us. Then we took off. We really enjoyed sitting out on the patio at our hotel looking at the ocean and just relaxing as well as walking outside holding hands and taking couple selfies. God arranged it so the annual car show was in town that weekend, so we really enjoyed looking at all of the classic automobiles.

Don't let your marriage get boring. Be or get creative. Find out what your partner's needs are. Also, couples should be making love not just having sex on a level of simply meeting a physical need. This takes time and planning on the part of both of you. I'm reminded of the phrase "the art of love making." If you think of a work of art, when the artist paints it, many layers of effort go into it. The artist doesn't just dip the brush into some paint and begin to throw the paint at the canvas. While this has been an artistic technique used by some artists recently, I do not feel that most of these end products get referred to as "works of art." We want our time coming together intimately to be beautiful, fulfilling, and full of emotion and meaning.

Calling All Wives: Look in the Mirror!

What can we wives do? Well, we can pay attention to our husbands and to ourselves. Here's an example. I was watching my favorite T.V. show, *Downton Abbey*, one Sunday night after my husband had gone to bed early. There was a part in the episode when Edith and her new editor were considering a new women's advice column to be run in the newspaper Edith owns. The editor began to read an example of the mysterious columnist's advice, "If your husband is showing signs of not being interested – try looking in the mirror!"

That line immediately struck me. Maybe I needed to do what the mystery columnist was advising. I wasn't happy at all to hear those words because it meant I had to do some reflecting on how I had been conducting myself lately. Was I becoming boring and fuddy-duddy? How was my appearance looking? Luckily, I had already started eating low-fat foods and had begun losing a few pounds. I also admitted to myself that I needed to buy some sexier lingerie. The very next day I purchased a few things at a very reasonable price. I think good colors are black, white, or red, with black being the best. However, it won't hurt to ask your husband what color he would like to see you wear. If you want to splurge a bit, you can shop at *Victoria's Secret* or *Soma*. However, I decided that night to get a few more sexy and cute pajamas and nighties for wearing at night.

In the booklets entitled *One Hundred and One Ways to Your Husband's Heart* and *One Hundred and*

One Ways to Your Wife's Heart, by Nick and Rosie Allan, Nick writes number 10 to wives, "Don't hesitate to change your appearance: try a new haircut, different shades of makeup, a switch in perfume, an unusual nightgown. Keep him guessing and interested."

Sometimes, you may not want to try a new haircut. But instead, you can try a different shade of hair color or even a sexy wig. Of course, I believe husbands do actually prefer us to wear our natural hair, so wigs should not become an all-the-time thing. We cannot expect to get a different and amazing result in our marriage relationship by continuing to do the same old boring things.

In Conclusion About Sex

Husbands need to coax their wives adequately and lovingly into lovemaking through conversation, affection, and gentle caressing, kissing, and touching. Wives also need to find ways to be thoughtful and kind towards their husbands. Creativity is helpful for sparking romance and sexual encounters. Husbands and wives need to discuss, study, and read Christian books together on the subject of how to better meet each other's needs. I recommend that you and your husband read all or parts of this chapter together. You can also ask if he minds you reading it to him. You can explain to your hubby that this will help you both experience more fulfillment in your intimate times together.

Pray about the right time to have the discussion with your husband. Also, pray about your sexual relationship with your husband. There is a prayer called "His Sexuality" in the book I mentioned earlier by Stormie Omartian.[2] There is also an excellent resource that goes through much detail and gives step-by-step moves of the sexual encounters between a husband and wife.[3]

Wives, God created sex to be thoroughly enjoyed within the context of marriage, so have fun with your husbands in this way. Remember, God wants you and your husband to be happy, free, and fulfilled in every aspect of your marriage and He should get the glory in your sexual relationship also. Bring every aspect of your marriage to Jesus and He will make sure to bless it. . Enjoy!

TANIA CHAPMAN SCOTT

Chapter Five

What Happened to My Prince Charming?

Prince Charming was the prince who swept Cinderella off her feet in the original Disney movie which came out in 1950. According to Disney Wiki, Prince Charming's name "suggests he is the prince of a faraway kingdom, known for his dashing and handsome air. On the night of a royal ball, Charming falls in love with a mysterious maiden. Before he could learn her name, the maiden flees the castle, leaving only a glass slipper behind. The enamored Charming thus vows to use the slipper to find and marry his true love" (disney.fandom.com, n.d., accessed September 21, 2022).

There have been 12 renditions of the Cinderella movie made from 1915 to 2021. That means women and girls have been watching some variation of the Cinderella story for over a century! For years, many of us carried within us expectations for a husband that were engrained in our hearts from watching the beautiful princess yearn for and find her handsome young prince. Ladies, he's fine, tall, and he's rich! But while I was praying about writing this chapter, God revealed to me the problem inherent in making this very desirable man the object of our hearts' desire.

The Holy Spirit said, "Prince Charming was just a man, albeit a fictional one." But since we're bringing him to life anyway, He went on to say, "Underneath your knight's shining armor is a man with flaws and strengths just like any other human being. He's like all other men whether rich, poor, tall, or short."

As little girls, we idealized Prince Charming. We built him up in our minds and then said to ourselves, "Yes! That's the man for me! He's got everything I want, and nothing of the things I don't want." So, we set out to find a husband who would meet those criteria without realizing that real people are multi-faceted.

Let's look at my handsome prince, Gordon. When I met him, he was in his mid-twenties. That means he had more than a quarter of a century of experiences influencing the man he was at that time. Could I possibly be able to limit him to some finite set of qualities or somehow believe that all of his qualities would meet my fantasy for a husband? However, the problem is that romanticized character I had created in my mind just doesn't exist.

So, let's now discuss some of the unrealistic expectations that are the leading causes of divorce. What are some of the unrealistic, unmet expectations we wives have acquired leading up to marriage? Dr. Karen Finn, who has been through a divorce herself and is a divorce and life coach, writes, "Almost all marriages are pregnant with unrealistic expectations and when these impractical expectations are left unmet, we start moving away from the marriage. These unrealistic expectations often stem from fairy tales, movies, magazines, articles, and even our family and friends. However, if we don't deal with our expectations ourselves, it can quickly eat away the connection and lead us down the path of divorce" ("How Unrealistic Expectations in Marriage Can Lead to a Divorce" themindsjournal.com, October 19, 2019).

Dr. Finn also added this statistic: According to a report published by the National Fatherhood Initiative in 2006, the organization conducted a national survey on Marriage in America, and "one of their findings was that 45% of divorced respondents said that unrealistic expectations in marriage by them and/or their spouse was a major contributor to the end of their marriage." Dr. Finn came to a logical conclusion: almost half of all divorces are caused "in major part because of unrealistic expectations."

Common Unrealistic Unspoken Expectations

What unrealistic expectations did you carry with you on your wedding day and on into your marriage? Here is a list of a few of the unrealistic and unspoken expectations a lot of us wives internalized. I chose the following top 5 mentioned in the above article because most of them I carried myself into my marriage. Let's take a look at them and see why they are not realistic.

1.   **Your spouse should complete you and make you happy**. As young women, we believe that once we get married, we will be so happy and feel content because we have found someone wonderful with whom to share our lives.

Why expectation #1 is unrealistic. The problem with this belief is that if you aren't already whole within yourself, no other person can accomplish this for you. The root of this unrealistic expectation is seen early on in a person's dating history. For example, during high school up until my early twenties, if I broke up with someone, I needed to start talking to someone else soon afterward. Why was this? In looking back, I believe it was because I didn't feel happy or complete within myself.

2.   You should spend all your free time together – just like you did when you fell in love. When I married Gordon, I can remember having this euphoria-like feeling whenever I was with him. I wanted to be with him all the time, even when I went shopping at my favorite department store.

Why expectation #2 is unrealistic. The problem with the belief that our husbands should be spending all or most of their free time with us is this: men tend to need down time or time spent with other guys – time to relax and debrief from work. They also like to participate in other activities that may not involve their wives. Early on, the way Gordon behaved when I asked him to go shopping with me pretty much took away that feeling I had of being so excited whenever I was with him. He was not fun to be with when we went shopping, so I said I would just be happier going by myself. And so, I lost the excitement I had initially. However, had I understood that realistically my husband didn't want to spend his free time watching me floating around Macy's for an hour or more, I would have saved myself (and him) from going through that unhappy experience. I also still love being with my hubby.

3.   You will be able to make your spouse change in the way you want him to.

This is a very common mistake that a lot of wives make. It is said that women get married, hoping to change their husband, while men get married, hoping their wife will never change (see the next unrealistic expectation). Women have been known to think, or even say to others, "I'm going to change that about him," or "Don't worry, he will change after we get married."

Why expectation #3 is unrealistic. The big problem with this one is that no one individual has the power to make someone change. As parents, we are even unable to change our adult children (and sometimes little children are resistant and strong-willed). Oftentimes, we are even unable to make changes within ourselves, without much prayer and God's help.

4.   Your spouse will never change. This sounds like the complete opposite of the previous unrealistic expectation; however, this one is focusing on the characteristics that we liked about our spouse in the past, and not wanting that to ever change. Husbands especially often expect their spouse to stay the same weight as they were when they first got married. And we wives expect our husbands to continue doing the things he did in the beginning of the relationship in order to win us over.

Why expectation #4 is unrealistic. The expectation that our husbands will not change at all is unrealistic. For example, I wanted my marriage – and my life – to somehow be like one of those movies in which the main characters keep reliving the same day over and over again! That is not realistic. Also, someone not wanting their spouse to ever change physically is unrealistic as well. Over time, everything must change. Both time and seasons bring about changes in relationships and in couples themselves. One of the biggest changes that takes place in a marriage is when we have children, or when a blended family comes together.

As I mentioned in chapter 4, I started noticing patterns in certain couples when Gordon and I were out and about. It seemed like married couples didn't act as romantic as couples that appeared to just be dating. I had started noticing that Gordon was sometimes not being as affectionate as he was at other times. I told Gordon that it seemed like men change after they get married. At the time, we were walking along the marina like we had done when everything had begun for us, back on our second date in Redondo Beach. Gordon then asked me what made me think that relationships don't change. He also said I had changed as well! I immediately started naming all of the ways that I had *not* changed, like working on keeping my weight down. But I too needed to do some self-reflection about getting back that loving feeling.

But still, from my side of things, no wife ever gets married thinking that one day her husband is going to start treating her differently. Yet, nonetheless, change happens quite frequently in marriage, and it's important to start having discussions as soon as we become aware of any shifting in treatment that makes us feel uncomfortable.

Furthermore, it certainly is unrealistic to believe our marriage will somehow stay the same without working on it and without paying attention to it along the way! We can work at keeping our marriage relationships fresh, full of love, and not boring. We can be more spontaneous and more affectionate. We can kiss each other more, make love more often, and do fun things like we used to when we first got married. We should pray about problem areas, asking God to restore and revive our marriage. We can read books like this one, get marriage counseling, or go to marriage retreats. We need to first make necessary changes within ourselves, and then start talking with our husband about what we would like to see us bring back to the marriage!

Unless your husband is experiencing an illness or an age-related health challenge, the expectation that he will not change the way he originally treated you, is realistic. Husbands and wives need to keep doing the things that made the other one want to get married in the first place.

5. Your spouse's life should revolve around you. I think that when we women get married, we imagine our husbands will live and breathe just to make us happy and show us that we are the most important person in their lives. We think, "How lucky they are to have married us." We want our husbands to appreciate us, and better yet, to show us their appreciation! This may be a legitimate desire to want this from our husbands, but it is an unrealistic and selfish one.

Why expectation #5 is unrealistic. For most

husbands, their wife is the most important person in their life; however, men show their appreciation for their wives differently than we would like them to. Most men's lives revolve around doing manly things, like providing for the home and family; doing the best they can at work, business, or church; and trying to make the world a better place—at least they're immediate community. Also remember, your husband had relationships with family members and friends years before you two got married. We cannot expect our husbands to totally abandon those relationships. Although their lives cannot possibly revolve exclusively around each other, married couples do need to prioritize their relationship above everyone else except Jesus. Husbands must leave their family members and cleave to their wives. And yet, this doesn't mean that their lives will revolve exclusively around their wives either.

Biblical Expectations for Husbands (and Wives Too)

In Part 5 of chapter one, I gave you a legitimate expectation that wives should expect from our husbands. Colossians 3:19 in the Amplified Bible says, "Husbands, love your wives [be affectionate and sympathetic with them] and do not be harsh or bitter or resentful toward them." We wives should expect this from our husbands because it is found right in the Word of God. After all, "Every Scripture is God-breathed (given by His inspiration) and profitable for instruction... for training in righteousness (in holy living, in conformity to God's will in *thought*, *purpose*, and *action*)" (2 Timothy 3:16 AMPC, emphasis added).

In the Amplified translations of the Bible, words in

parenthesis or brackets are from the original meaning of key words in Hebrew (OT) or Greek (NT). Notice it says "…for training in righteousness (in holy living, in conformity to God's will *in thought, purpose, and action.*" We are to know what God's word says and allow it to help us to align ourselves with His will, in our thoughts, purposes, and actions. So, let's make the Word of God our guide for determining what our primary expectations should be from our husbands.

Now, sister friend, I want us to look at the realistic expectations that relate to each of the unrealistic expectations discussed above. I have listed what the Bible has to say about the above expectations that some of us may have been walking around with before we first got married. Some of these thoughts are more than likely still there in the recesses of our minds. I want us to excavate the unrealistic expectations and expose them to the truth of God's Word that tells us we shall know the truth, and the truth will make us free. Let's get free!

1.   **Only Jesus can truly complete you and give you peace**. The Bible clearly states that Jesus, or the word, is where we should look for fulfillment and to be made whole or complete. This is contrary to believing that our spouse will somehow complete us. Another human being will inevitably let us down. Jesus will never fail us because He represents God in all of His fullness. "For in Christ lives all the fullness of God in a human body. So, you also are complete through your union with Christ,

who is the head over every ruler and authority"
(Colossians 2:9 – 10 NLT).

We often use the word "union" to depict a
marriage. But here in Colossians, the word "union"
describes becoming one with Christ when we accept
Him in our hearts, as Lord and Savior. This is how we
become complete. Have you ever thought you were
somehow "less than" or lacking in some way? If so,
that is a false belief. This scripture proves Jesus
represents God in all His fullness, and we became full
or complete when we were united with Him! That is a
revelation for every Christian woman to know. Put it on
our bumper sticker as a reminder if needed! Praise God,
it's true because it's in the Word of God! Do you think
it's a coincidence that the Bible calls the church of
Jesus Christ His bride? I don't think so.

Christ has helped me to feel complete. After a few
times of feeling frustrated because I wanted Gordon to
act differently, I realized that taking things into my own
hands wasn't getting me anywhere. Instead, I began to
take the problem to God in prayer, casting my cares on
God, by telling Him whatever had gone on between
Gordon and me. During those times of just pouring my
heart out to God, I began to notice the peace of God
would fill me as I was praying. By the time I was done,
I felt that everything was going to be okay! And I was
no longer upset. I had total peace, knowing God and
Jesus love me, and knowing my prayers had been
heard.

In John 14:28 AMPC, Jesus says, "Peace I leave
with you; My [perfect] peace I give to you; not as the
world gives do I give to you. Do not let your heart be

troubled, nor let it be afraid. [Let My perfect peace calm you in every circumstance and give you courage and strength for every challenge.]" That is just one way Jesus can make you feel whole, calm, peaceful, and free from worry or lack.

> **2.   Husbands need to be "sharpened" by wise friends, and they need time to rest.** Unlike believing our husbands should spend all of their free time with us, the Bible speaks of a man's need to be "sharpened" by the good counsel of his friends. This actually applies to everyone, male and female. Proverbs, which is full of wise counsel, states, "As iron sharpens iron, so one man sharpens [and influences] another [through discussion]" (Proverbs 27:17 AMP).

This scripture speaks about the importance of each one of us spending time with friends and receiving influence from them. Husbands and wives should be each other's best friends and be able to counsel each other in some areas. However, in other areas, we are not effective counselors for our spouses. We can talk to our close friends about some things we wouldn't talk with our spouse about. For example, I noticed some years ago that Gordon preferred to discuss work-related problems and issues with a close friend of his. One of the pastors at our church spoke about this at a marriage seminar a few years ago. He said, "Be incredibly grateful that your spouse has friends who can meet needs that you can't meet. Find ways to celebrate what you can't share, but also what you can share." (Joel & Marie Holmes, Marriage Seminar, February 8, 2014)

So, this should definitely help us understand that our husbands will not be spending all of their free time with us. A warning here though: Husbands should not be going out to clubs or bars with their friends. There will be drinking and single women there, and those two things are not a wise combination. It's best if your husband's friends are male, Christian, and preferably married. They don't have to hang out in bars to talk with friends. Your husband can hang out with his friends at sporting events, the golf course, bike rides, coffee shops, over lunch, while on a double date with you and another couple, during family gatherings, or even at a party that you attend together. Single men can be around your husband, but your husband should be a positive influence on them. The same rule holds for you and your girlfriends.

Another biblical expectation for our husbands is that we should expect them to need to rest, as opposed to going around with us everywhere. This is especially necessary if they have a stressful, mentally exhausting, physically demanding job, or get up early every morning. In Matthew 11:28, Jesus says, "Come to Me, all *you* who labor and are heavy laden, and I will give you rest."

Gordon's job can be very stressful. One way I've noticed that he "comes to Jesus" for rest and relaxation is that he will play music from a playlist of Christian artists while he is working on his classic Chevy truck. That's usually what he likes to do on Saturdays. Allow your husband to rest. Encourage and pray for him to make Jesus a part of his resting routine.

Getting outdoors and experiencing nature is also a good way to get in touch with God. I have heard golfing is extremely relaxing. Sometimes, our husbands may want to just binge on their favorite television show. If these things allow them to take their minds off of the daily stresses of work and all of the rigor of being a provider and leader of the household for a few hours a week, then we should give them the space to regroup and regenerate and not begrudge them of doing it.

However, husbands need to be careful about "checking out" of the marriage through excessive relaxation activities when they are at home. If you have noticed this taking place, make sure you haven't allowed your husband to become bored or under stimulated within the marriage. (You may want to review chapter 4 on this point!)

3.   God is the best agent for change, so put away your magic wand. Wanting to somehow make our spouse change the way we want them to change, most often leads our spouses to view us as controlling and perhaps self-centered.

In 1 Corinthians, chapter 13, known as the "love chapter," the scripture gives some criteria for true love:

"Love is patient and kind. Love is not jealous or boastful or proud or rude. *It does not demand its own way.* It is not irritable, and it keeps no record of being wronged. It does not rejoice about injustice but rejoices whenever the truth wins out. Love never gives up, never loses faith, is always hopeful, and endures through every circumstance." (1Corinthians 13:4 – 7 NLT, emphasis added).

If our husbands have characteristics that do need to be changed, God is the best one to change them. God told the children of Israel this about Himself, through the prophet Isaiah:

> "Do not remember the former things or ponder the things of the past. Listen carefully, I am about to do a new thing, now it will spring forth; will you not be aware of it? I will even put a road in the wilderness, rivers in the desert. ... Yet you have not called on Me [in prayer and worship], O Jacob; but you have grown weary of Me, O Israel" (Isaiah 43: 18 – 19, 22 AMP).

God was saying here, He is able to do the new thing we desperately need, and when he does it, we will know He did it because the outcome is going to be miraculous! But He goes on to say Israel had not even bothered to go to Him with their problems. We should learn from this that God knows how to bring about change; therefore, if we want something to change in our spouses, a real good approach would be to take some time and pray about it first, before we even bring it up to our husbands.

Another verse of scripture that speaks of God's ability to get things done is found in Ecclesiastes.

> "I know that whatever God does, it endures forever; nothing can be added to it nor can anything be taken from it, for God does it so that men will fear *and* worship Him [with awe-filled reverence, knowing that He is God]" (Ecclesiastes 3:14 AMP).

Stormy Omartian's book *The Power of A Praying Wife* says, "Our goal must not be to get our husbands to do what we want, but rather to release them to God so He can get them to do what He wants. Distinguish carefully between what is truly right and wrong. If it doesn't fall clearly into either of those categories, keep your personal opinions to yourself. Or pray about them and then as the Lord leads, reveal them for calm discussion." [1]

4.   God is the only One who will never change. When I was praying about which scripture in the Bible addresses the unrealistic expectation that our spouses will never change, the following scripture in Malachi, popped into my spirit. "For I am the LORD, I do not change [but remain faithful to My covenant with you]; that is why you, O sons of Jacob, have not come to an end" (Malachi 3:6 AMP).

When I read the above verse where the Lord says He remained faithful to His covenant with the children of Israel, I thought about the way some husbands and wives do not remain faithful to their covenant with their spouses. This, of course, is the ultimate and saddest change a married person can make.

But God on the other hand can always be counted on to remain faithful to His word and to His covenant with us! Now that is an amazing fact to hold onto whenever we begin to doubt God. Unlike any human being, God is the personification of faithfulness to what He has said, and He is also faithful to complete what He has started. God's supernatural commitment to never change should help us see that no human being can ever meet that criterion.

5.   The head does not revolve around anyone else. Even though I was a math teacher for more than 20 years, and have a somewhat analytical mind, I was never a big science buff. One thing I do understand, though, is how the planets in our solar system revolve around the sun and not vice versa. When I think of our married relationships and our families with which God has blessed us, the husband is likened to the sun because he is leader of the household and the one who should be doing the best he can to move heaven and earth to provide for his family and be the leader. The family revolves around him and not vice versa.

The Bible says, "For the husband is head of the wife, as also Christ is head of the church; and He is the Savior of the body. Therefore, just as the church is subject to Christ, so *let* the wives *be* to their own husbands in everything" (Ephesians 5:23 – 24).

Just like you would never want the sun to lose its strength and power, you should never want your husband to lose his strength and power. Although, it's not a pure analogy I'm making here; nonetheless, I don't think we truly want our husbands revolving around us. Most women who are able to get their husbands to do that, eventually lose some respect for their husbands.

By comparing our own contrived expectations,

based on whatever source, to what the Word of God says, I have attempted in this chapter to help us learn how to separate realistic expectations from the ones that are unrealistic and thereby unattainable.

TANIA CHAPMAN SCOTT

Chapter Six

He's Not Meeting My Needs, Somebody Else Will!

The temptations in your life are no different from what others experience. And God is faithful. He will not allow the temptation to be more than you can stand. When you are tempted, he will show you a way out so that you can endure. (1Corinthians 10:13 TLB)

※

When your needs and expectations are not being met, thoughts can easily begin to enter your mind. There's disappointment because you didn't walk down the aisle anticipating that your future husband was going to stop meeting your needs, so you start toying around with the idea of someone else making you happy. Feelings of emptiness flood your body that can all seem quite irrational, but you are desperate. Like a person lost in the desert without any water, you begin grasping for ways to quench your thirst. Looking for something that will satisfy you, thoughts and feelings of attraction for a co-worker, your best friend's husband, or even someone you barely even know begin to bombard your mind. The devil wants you to believe you can get your fix of happiness by going through a "drive-thru for unhappy wives" and get a "quickie" or an instant love affair to somehow make you feel better.

The inordinate feelings are just some of Satan's strategies to try to destroy your marriage by tempting you. In the Tyler Perry movie *Temptation: Confessions of a Marriage Counselor*, a marriage counselor tells a female client her sad confession of her own marriage, under the disguise that she is talking about her sister Judith's marriage. In the story, after marrying her childhood sweetheart, Judith becomes dissatisfied with her husband. He forgets her birthday and fails to notice her when she changes her appearance. Enter a handsome wealthy man into her workplace. He talks to her, questioning some of her core values, and then tells her that her sex life with her husband is boring. He also notices her and woos her with flowers and compliments. Even though her husband attempts to fight for her, Judith chooses the other man. They have an affair, and it doesn't end well for Judith at all. She ends up with HIV, gets a divorce, and watches her husband move on to another wife and a happy life.

The seven stages I saw in the progression of the affair that resulted in the destruction of Judith's marriage can all too easily become stages for you if you allow the enemy to infiltrate your unhappy marriage.

1. A Chance Encounter – The enemy will present an opportunity by chance for you to be tempted. For example, right when you are mad or disappointed with your husband, an old boyfriend messages you on Facebook to see how you've been doing, or your girlfriend invites you to go out to a club and a guy keeps flirting with you.

2. Conversation – The person sent in to tempt you will say something that you, in turn,

allow to become a lingering thought in your mind. There's a quote by Martin Luther, my mom always told me, "You cannot keep birds from flying over your head, but you can keep them from building a nest in your hair." Every sinful action begins with a sinful or incorrect thought.

    3.   Comparing/Competition with Your Mate – The tempter goes out of his way to compete with the intended target's spouse. He presents himself as someone who is willing to do everything your spouse is not willing to do, or just doesn't take the time to do. This step can also take the form of comparisons in your own mind between the other person and your husband.

    4.   Collusion – This is when members of the opposite team conspire to cheat. And this is exactly what people do when they decide to do any of the following with someone who has made advances towards them, or to whom they are attracted physically:

        a. Go on a business trip together.

        b. Go on lunch/dinner dates together.

        c. Exchange texts, phone calls, or social media messages.

        d. Be alone together.

    5.   Carnal Knowledge – This is the stage when Satan gets his victims to go through with a sexual act with someone to whom they are not married.

6.   Cohabitation – This is when the married person leaves the spouse to live with the lover. It is a sinful state to be in and God does not bless it because it is done outside of seeking His will. It is an action taken to seek only what you want, not what God wants, because God will not have you disobey His Word in order for you to be "happy." In Jeremiah 3:20, God says, "Surely, as a wife treacherously departs from her husband, so have you dealt treacherously with Me, O house of Israel."

7.   Conclusion – According to hackspirit.com, extra-marital affairs usually come to an end within six months or less.[1] Oftentimes, one person will have another affair, and move on, or they will just break up because the relationship was based on lust and not love. Sometimes, people will return to their spouse. When people do remain in relationships that started as affairs, it can be plagued with trust issues.[2]

While the above stages are based on fictional characters from a movie, it is still a good illustration of how Satan can destroy your marriage through temptation. Even if you know that you would never do anything like this, please read on because "most people are surprised by their own behavior at the start of an affair" ("*26 Surprising Statistics on Cheating Spouses,*" healthresearchfunding.org, n.d.). Additionally, you may be able to help someone else.

According to an article on hackspirit.com, the following is true about why people cheat on their spouses:

> "Obviously every woman is different. That
> said, women tend to cheat for very different
> reasons than men. In general, women
> cheat when they feel a lack of intimacy and feel
> ignored by their partner, whereas men are more
> visual and tend to cheat due to immediate
> temptation".[3]

If our husbands aren't giving us the affection, attention, or quality time we need, we can feel unimportant, ignored, empty, and doubtful as to whether or not they are still in love with us. That's when the enemy can step in and start causing us to dwell on something our husbands have done or not done. Satan will try to keep us dwelling on the perception that our spouse has failed to make us feel loved and cherished.

It is biblical to want to feel cherished by your husband, because the Bible commands husbands to do it in Ephesians 5:

> "Even so husbands should *and* are morally
> obligated to love their own wives as [being in a
> sense] their own bodies. He who loves his own
> wife loves himself. For no one ever hated his
> own body, but [instead] he nourishes *and*
> protects and cherishes it, just as Christ does the
> church, because we are members (parts) of His
> body." (Ephesians 5: 28 – 31 AMP)

In Willard F. Harley's book, *His Needs, Her Needs*, the author introduces the concept of a love bank. A love bank is a subconscious accounting of the "deposits" being made into us by our spouse, as well as the "withdrawals" that reduce our emotional feelings of love. Husbands can essentially make such deposits by showing affection to their wives—a vital component of a happy marriage. Your husband makes deposits to your love bank when he greets you with a hug or a kiss when he comes home, talks to you, listens without looking at his cellphone or computer, puts down the remote, tells you that you look nice, etc. On the other hand, each time he fails to show you the affection, attention, or communication you need from him, he is unconsciously making a withdrawal from your love bank account.

To illustrate how withdrawals are made from a wife's account, Farley talks about a couple named Jane and Richard. Richard was the strong silent type. When they were first dating, there was strong chemistry. "Dates with Richard felt exciting, and when he held her in his arms the passion level went right off the scale... However, after just a few months of marriage, the passion began to pall. Jane started noticing something a bit odd: Whenever she cuddled up for a hug or a little kiss, Richard became sexually aroused almost immediately. Almost without exception physical contact led straight to the bedroom." [4]

Richard's strong silent type personality also led him to be moody, non-communicative, and inattentive towards Jane. Due to the lowered balance in her love bank, Jane allowed herself to be seduced by a coworker. He started by giving Jane a hug every day. She enjoyed the hugs and began to look forward to them, and they ultimately ended up in an affair.

What could Jane have done differently, to avoid falling into Satan's trap? Remember, that Satan especially wants to ruin marriages because it is God's creation. And if he can mess up a Christian marriage, all the better, because then that is a bad reflection on God. One thing Jane could have done is to pray about the problem, and then speak in a non-confrontational manner with her husband about her needs not being met. In *The Power of A Praying Wife,* Stormie Omartian says: "Affection isn't at the top of a man's priority list because men often see sex and affection as being the same. A woman's greatest need is for affection. If you are in a marriage that lacks it, pray for the Holy Spirit's transformation." [5]

An Unfaithful Wife from the Book of Proverbs

Now, I want to tell you about another woman, one who is found in the Bible in the book of Proverbs. She is not as well-known, as her counterpart – the Proverbs 31 woman. In Proverbs 7, we see the picture of a woman who has set out to the streets to find a lover.

"For at the window of my house I looked out through my lattice. And among the naive [the inexperienced and gullible], I saw among the youths a young man lacking [good] sense, passing through the street near her corner; and he took the path to her house in the twilight, in the evening; in the black and dark night. And there a woman met him, dressed as a prostitute and sly *and* cunning of heart. She was boisterous and rebellious; she would not stay at home. At times *she was* in the streets, at times in the market places, lurking *and* setting her ambush at every corner. So, she caught him and kissed him

and with a brazen *and* impudent face she said to him, "I have peace offerings with me; today I have paid my vows. So I came out to meet you [that you might share with me the feast of my offering], diligently I sought your face and I have found you. I have spread my couch with coverings *and* cushions of tapestry, with colored fine linen of Egypt. I have perfumed my bed with myrrh, aloes, and cinnamon. Come, let us drink our fill of love until morning; let us console *and* delight ourselves with love. For my husband is not at home. He has gone on a long journey; he has taken a bag of money with him, and he will come home on the appointed day.'"
(Proverbs 7: 6 – 20, AMP)

What has led this wife to take such careless and ungodly actions? Some would be surprised to find that this woman is actually married. I know I was surprised. However, a word used in verse 18 led me to a conclusion. The woman says to the naïve young man, "Come… let us **console** *and* delight ourselves with love." "Console" means to "comfort (someone) in the time of grief or disappointment." A synonym that is listed for console is "**solace**," and in the King James version, it says "… let us **solace ourselves** with loves." So, I concluded that the Proverbs 7 woman became disillusioned, at some point in her marriage, and took it upon herself to seek comfort in another man's arms.

Unfortunately, wives have sought comfort in another man's arms, for years. But the problem with this is the woman trying to make up for some deficiency in her marriage or relationship by taking on various lovers, is in fact putting herself in a worse predicament. Now this married woman is being referred to as a "prostitute," because she has become so desperate, that she has taken to the streets and the marketplaces to find someone to be with and comfort her. Additionally, affairs can end with "love children" being born, violent revenge at the hand of either the husband or the lover, and sometimes murders occur as a result of affairs.

A family member told me about a Christian couple, where the wife was having multiple affairs. The couple had married after being childhood sweethearts and lived in a small town in the Midwest where everyone knew each other. The wife ended up being murdered at the motel where she was rendezvousing with one of her lovers. But there's a twist in the story because the cheating wife ended up being killed, not by her enraged husband, but by another jealous lover! Often, the choice to cheat doesn't end well because it represents sin as well as the works of the enemy's influence over your life. The Bible says, "There is a way that seems right to a man (woman), but its end is the way of death" (Proverbs 14:12).

While reading this sad tale of a woman whose life has gone astray, I couldn't help but wonder where exactly the Proverbs 7 woman's husband is while all of this is taking place. Verse 19 says her husband is away from home on a long journey, and his wife tells her perspective lover that he will return at an appointed time. Here, the word "journey" comes from the Hebrew word "dherekh" meaning literally "a going, walk, journey, way, path, road, mode, manner, course, way of life, lot in life, worship." When I began to research this word, I thought I might see some reference to this being a work-related trip. However, I found no indication that this was a journey a man took for the purpose of working. So, this journey could very well have been this woman's husband just off doing his thing. Afterall, the passage mentions her husband took a bag of money apparently for extravagant spending, or perhaps gambling, or whatever men did in those days.

Contrary to the Proverbs 7 woman's decision to let her husband's actions change the course of her life, we must not allow our husband's actions- or our dissatisfaction - to change who we are, and thereby lose our blessings. It's clear that she was a religious woman and followed some of the religious practices of her day, but it takes more than being religious to be a true woman of God. We must have an intimate relationship with God and seek His will for our lives.

In a Focus on the Family blog post, Jim Daly writes:

"...Proverbs 7 is a cautionary tale: when you either don't understand or choose to reject God's Word about who you are designed to be, you'll search for the answers wherever – and from whomever – you can find them.

You're especially at risk of drifting in the wrong direction if your marriage isn't going so well. You and your husband may be locked in conflict. Or maybe the two of you feel miles apart even when you're sleeping right next to each other. Maybe your struggle has grown so deep you've contemplated looking outside your marriage for answers that soothe you and fill up the emptiness inside.

Maybe you've already taken that step.

Wherever – or from whomever – you've sought for answers to your uncertainty, one thing you can know for sure: those temporary fixes will only deepen the emptiness you feel." ("Two Women of the Proverbs," Daly Focus: Jim Daly's Blog, jimdaly.focusonthefamily.com, March 15, 2016).

Stay True to Who God Says You Are

If you have experienced similar feelings as the Proverbs 7 Woman—or Judith, or Jane—I want to tell you that I empathize with how you may be feeling or may have felt in the past. Having been married for 32 years, I would be lying if I pretended I haven't ever had such feelings as these women. Even fantasizing that Denzel is your man qualifies as a sinful thought! But I can thankfully say I have never acted on the temptation to fool around on my husband, to make me happy. I will be darned if I let someone else change who I am in Christ. I am a pretty loyal person, and I just could not live with the idea of having an affair on my husband— someone who I made a vow to be faithful to.

Three of the characteristics of the Proverbs 31 woman are virtue, faithfulness, and reverence ("*17 Characteristics of A Proverbs 31 Woman*," www.theodysseyonline.com, Bella Mitchell, September 27, 2016). These characteristics are found in verses 10, 11 and 12 of Proverbs 31 as follows:

"An excellent woman [one who is spiritual, capable, intelligent, and virtuous], who is he who can find her? Her value is more precious than jewels *and* her worth is far above

rubies *or* pearls. The heart of her husband trusts in her [with secure confidence],
And he will have no lack of gain. She comforts, encourages, *and* does him only good and not evil all the days of her life." (Proverbs 31:10 – 12 AMP)

And I really love this next passage from the Bible in 1 Peter 3:

In the same way, you wives, be submissive to your own husbands [subordinate, not as inferior, but out of respect for the responsibilities entrusted to husbands and their accountability to God, and so partnering with them] so that even if some do not obey the word [of God], they may be won over [to Christ] without discussion by the *godly* lives of their wives, when they see your modest and respectful behavior [together with your devotion and appreciation—love your husband, encourage him, and enjoy him as a blessing from God]. (1Peter 3:1 – 3 AMPC)

God is the only One who is able to supply our every need. So even though our husbands sometimes do things that can make us very frustrated, as true women of God, we cannot go doing things that are contrary to the integrity within us and what the Bible says we are. We have to run to our heavenly Father with all of our needs. God calls Himself Jehovah Jireh, the one Who sees our needs and provides for them. He knows exactly what you need simply because He created us. Sometimes, we don't even know exactly what we need ourselves.

We have to surrender to Him one hundred percent and give our husband and marriage over to Him, entrusting Him to work on both the husband and the wife. In the meantime, we must live our best life which is to live in the will of God. This will happen as we read the Word and pray daily, making sure we are being open and transparent with our heavenly Father. A great way to start out your day is with devotionals that include daily scriptures to read and life application suggestions. I read a devotional Bible to read through the Bible in one year. I write out the scriptures that minister to me each day. I also pray.

Look to God's word to find out what His perfect Will is for your life. Romans confirms this fact:

> "And do not be conformed to this world [any longer with its superficial values and customs], but be transformed *and* progressively changed [as you mature spiritually] by the renewing of your mind [focusing on godly values and ethical attitudes], so that you may prove [for yourselves] what the will of God is, that which is good and acceptable and perfect [in His plan and purpose for you]." (Romans 12:2 AMP)

How do we renew our minds and focus on godly values and ethical attitudes as it states in the amplified version above? The most rational place would be God's word. That's where He has caused His prophets, disciples, and His Son to record His word and His will for His children. Most parents know and love the verse of scripture from Proverbs which states to: Train up a child in the way he (or she) should go, and when they are old, they will not depart from it. The same way you would train up a child to take the correct path when he or she is an adult, is the way we need to continue training our own minds after we are adults – so we can be mature in the faith, learn, grow, and achieve God's perfect will for our lives. Of course, this process also includes much prayer and surrendering our lives to the Father to achieve this.

What Makes You Happy?

The truth is, no one outside of ourselves can truly make us happy, but God. It says this in Colossians, chapter 2:

> "For in Christ there is all of God in a human body; *so you have everything when you have Christ,*" (Colossians 2:9 – 10a TLB)

Your happiness should also come from within yourself. We must also find out what will bring us true and lasting happiness. One of the things that I am the proudest of about my daughters, is that they know what makes them happy. And they do not search for happiness from being in a relationship alone or having a boyfriend. My oldest daughter is full of wisdom and insight, she really enjoys writing. and her newsletters and blogs have been shared on several websites. She has written her own book, having graduated with a degree in screenwriting. She is a "foodie" who enjoys rock climbing and doing yoga. She owns her natural hair journey, has travelled to Europe, has her own unique style, and loves to thrift although she also likes sustainable clothing. She is an independent spirit and does her job well. She moved 2,500 miles away from home at the age of 22 to pursue a dream.

My youngest daughter is smart as a whip. A music enthusiast, she's a UCLA grad having majored in music history. She loves dancing, goes to at least 4 or 5 concerts per year, and enjoys taking road trips with her friends. She sports her natural hair; loves thrifting, crocheting, and repurposing; and remakes clothing from thrifted items. She owns three sewing machines and can be found sewing away in her room after work, making outfits and handbags for her friends, and filming her process for social media.

Both of my girls have their own websites. In short, they rock, and I would love to be like them when I grow up! I pray that after they get married, they will continue doing the things they love—the things that make them unique.

What makes you happy and what do you love to do? Never let anything or anyone make you forget about what brings you joy. Those activities make up part of who you are, and who you were prior to setting eyes on your husband. You could have discovered new interests after you got married. For example, while I discovered my love of singing as a child, I started writing in my thirties. I also discovered later on in life, that I love being a creator on social media, and I love teaching the Word of God. God called me to serve Him after I got married, but I got saved while in middle school, even though I was not raised in church.

A Virtuous and Talented Wife from the Book of Proverbs

The Proverbs 31 Woman is in the Bible as a reference for Christian men and women. She serves as a picture of what a godly woman is capable of doing with her life. She was not a real person, rather, a king's mother wrote this list of qualities for her son's future wife, when he was still a young prince. She serves as a shining example for all Christian wives. She is virtuous, kind, faithful, full of wisdom, and industrious. She is a philanthropist, a businesswoman, a seamstress, a chef specializing in international cuisine, an early riser, an effective human resource manager, and a real estate investor, among other things! And if all of that were not enough, she is also a mother and a wife! The Bible describes her many talents as follows:

"She finds wool and flax and busily spins it. She is like a merchant's ship, bringing her food from afar. She gets up before dawn to prepare breakfast for her household and plan the day's work for her servant girls. She goes to inspect a field and buys it; with her earnings she plants a vineyard. She is energetic and strong, a hard worker. She makes sure her dealings are profitable; her lamp burns late into the night. Her hands are busy spinning thread, her fingers twisting fiber. She extends a helping hand to the poor and opens her arms to the needy. She has no fear of winter for her household, for everyone has warm clothes. She makes her own bedspreads. She dresses in fine linen and purple gowns. She makes belted linen garments and sashes to sell to the merchants. She is clothed with strength and dignity, and she laughs without fear of the future. When she speaks, her words are wise, and she gives instructions with kindness. She carefully watches everything in her household and suffers nothing from laziness. Her children stand and bless her. Her husband praises her, 'There are many virtuous and capable women in the world, but you surpass them all!" " (Proverbs 31: 13 – 22, 24 – 29 NLT)

As you can see, this woman of God pictured in the Proverbs was a busy, capable, talented, and a strong woman in her own right! From looking at this woman's life, no one could ever say she was defined in any way as just being a wife. No, she had many facets and layers to her life! The woman of Proverbs 31 ministers to me because she is her own woman, with her own interests, talents, and purpose. She was a woman who feared God and was faithful to her husband, making him and her children very proud! Let us strive to bear some resemblance to this godly wife in the book of Proverbs.

What If My Spouse is in Ill Health or Doesn't Take Proper Care of Himself?

I was speaking with a friend of the family who told me her husband had not been taking good care of his health, despite her telling him that he needs to do better. She has now become his caregiver because of his poor health. She has found it difficult to continue to live with him and has since moved out to a place of her own. She hasn't confided in me, but I am aware that it is difficult to impossible to remain intimate with her husband. I am also aware of women whose husbands are unable to have a sexual relationship with them because of erectile dysfunction for reasons unknown to the couple or due to some medical condition.

What is a wife to do in this situation? These are women who have very real physical needs and desire to be intimate physically with their husbands. Yet sometimes spouses do not take proper care of themselves. This results in health problems or serious obesity which creates a sexual deficit in the marriage relationship. The healthy spouse may want to seek intimacy from someone other than the mate.

I fully understand the dilemma people face in this situation. But I also know God is a God of possibilities, and nothing shall be impossible with Him (Luke 1:37). We must first take all of our problems to God. In Hebrews, chapter 4, the Bible says, "For we do not have a High Priest who cannot sympathize with our weaknesses, but was in all *points* tempted as *we are, yet* without sin. Let us therefore come boldly to the throne of grace, that we may obtain mercy and find grace to help in time of need" (Hebrews 4: 15 – 16).

God is all knowing – Omniscient. He is all powerful – Omnipotent. And yes, He is everywhere at the same time – Omnipresent. So, He already knows what we are dealing with before we even pray. But not only that, God has the power to do something about it! Let's pray:

"Our gracious and merciful Heavenly Father, we (I) come boldly before Your throne of grace to receive Your mercy and grace in our time of great need. Lord, today I bring my marriage before you. Lord, we have been having difficulty coming together intimately as husband and wife, and I know that this is not your will, or your plan, for us. Lord, I ask that You expose, remove, and reveal any and all hinderances to my husband and I being able to enjoy each other physically, as You have provided in Your word in 1 Corinthians 7. Lord,

I bind the enemy away from my husband's body, I bind sickness and disease away from him, and us not being able to have an intimate sexual relationship together. Lord, I ask You to bind this problem in heaven, in Your Son Jesus' Name. Father, I ask You to bind any sickness that has come against my husband's body, in Jesus Christ of Nazareth's name. And I loose Your healing Power – Your healing virtue – to flow over my husband, right now, from the top of his head to the very soles of his feet. Father, I loose Your anointing over my marriage bed and over my husband's body and my body as well. Lord, I ask You to loose Your healing power and healing virtue over us in heaven as well. Lord, I ask you to do a mighty miracle in my marriage which will enable my husband and I to resume making love, in Your Son's Mighty Name – Jesus Christ of Nazareth! Amen and Amen!"

After praying this prayer the first time, continue to pray it daily, however replace "I *ask* You …" with "Lord, I *thank* you …." Also ask God to help you and your husband to get creative in the meantime, with being intimate with each other. Ask your husband to kiss you more, to hold you and touch you where you need to be touched and held. Amen?

A New Husband Will Likely Only Be a Temporary Fix

No matter how many different mates we seek out to bring us happiness, only God—El Shaddai—will be sufficient to meet our needs. The statistics show the chances of divorce go up from first marriages to second marriages, to third marriages (*"Fascinating Remarriage Statistics,"* by Goldberg Jones, www.goldbergjones-sandiego.com, August 15, 2022).

It would make logical sense that when attempting to find happiness in another spouse, the likelihood of some of the same problems—or perhaps just completely different ones that may even be worse than what you experienced in the first marriage—will resurface or surface in the second and the third marriages.

Therefore, it's wise to take the problems in our marriage to the All Knowing and All Sufficient One Who is able to do exceedingly and abundantly above all that we could ever ask or imagine (Ephesians 3:20)! And read books like this one and others that I've mentioned herein, as well as get counselling if necessary.

Chapter Seven

Lord, Will You Please Change This Man?

"My thoughts are nothing like your thoughts," says the Lord. "And my ways are far beyond anything you could imagine. For just as the heavens are higher than the earth, so my ways are higher than your ways and my thoughts higher than your thoughts. (Isaiah 55:8 – 9 NLT)

Women especially, go into relationships saying to themselves, "Yeah, I'm going to change this man. He'll come around. He'll need a little bit of training, but he won't be able to resist my strategies. He will obey what he's told!"

When you were still dating your husband, you may have noticed something a little "troubling" about him. But there were so many positives, you may have ignored the negative things that you didn't really want to deal with in the first place. For example, after Gordon and I got engaged, I noticed he wasn't very talkative at times. We even had an argument about it. But I let it pass, thinking that everything would work out, or maybe he would magically change.

Early in our marriage, I would end up telling God about my husband and asking Him to please change him! I would have these long, detailed complaining sessions with God that went essentially like this:

> "Lord, I'm tired of how Gordon does such and such and I need You to speak to him and tell him all of the things he's doing wrong because he doesn't want to do what I need him to do. Jesus, please show Gordon everything that he needs to do better. He's just doing his thing and acting like he doesn't care about what I need him to do. Lord, I just want to be happy, so I need You to please tell Gordon this time, because I'm done trying to tell him. Please forgive me for sounding disrespectful. I'm just tired and I need You to help this man to change! In Jesus' Name, Amen."

Be Honest with God

If this prayer sounds a little familiar, then at least I have the comfort of being in good company. Hopefully, you can see some humor in the way I was praying. In looking back on how I was approaching God, I wasn't asking God anything. What I was really doing was telling Him what I needed Him to do. It's funny that I thought I could get God to answer such a prayer. I think I was so frustrated in my marriage that I just wanted to pour my heart and soul out to my Heavenly Father. Much like a daughter would to her earthly father, in hopes that he would just fix the situation. In "The Power of a Praying Wife," author Stormie Omartian gives some encouraging advice on this topic:

> "The first thing to do is to be completely

honest with God. In order to break down the walls in our hearts and smash the barriers that stop communication, we have to be totally up front with the Lord about our feelings. We don't have to "pretty it up" for Him. He already knows the truth. He just wants to see if we're willing to admit it and confess it as disobedience to His ways. If so, He then has a heart with which He can work."[1]

It's comforting to know, that God isn't mad at us when we come boldly to Him sharing our marriage challenges and frustrations. But we should stay mindful of not lingering on the negative too long. As I reflect now on the way I prayed for Gordon in those early months and years of our marriage, I realize not only was I approaching God with an incorrect attitude – by trying to tell Him what to do – but I was also not considering what I needed to change. I was focusing only on Gordon's shortcomings and thinking only of my needs and not what Gordon needed. Philippians chapter 4 tells us:

> "Do not be anxious *or* worried about anything, but in everything [every circumstance and situation] by prayer and petition *with thanksgiving*, continue to make your [specific] requests known to God. And the peace of God [that peace which reassures the heart, …] which transcends all understanding, ...stands guard over your hearts and your minds in Christ Jesus [is yours]. (Philippians 4:6 – 7 AMP, emphasis added)

Notice the passage says we are to pray "with thanksgiving." It is difficult to keep complaining about my situation while also being thankful that God is going to give me what I'm praying for.

Be Positive

Paul must have known a lot of women would be praying for their husbands, so he added the reminder to stay positive at the end of this great lesson on prayer in Philippians:

> "Finally, believers, *whatever is true, whatever is honorable and worthy of respect,* whatever is right *and* confirmed by God's word, *whatever* is *pure and wholesome, whatever is lovely and brings peace, whatever is admirable and of good repute*; *if there is any excellence, if there is anything worthy of praise, think continually on these things* [center your mind on them, and implant them in your heart]."
> (Philippians 4:8 AMP, emphasis added)

A fun fact about me is my blood type is "B Positive." Surely God knew I would need an extra little reminder to stay positive – especially in my marriage! James chapter five also admonishes us not to complain about our fellow believers in Christ:

> "Do not complain against one another, believers, so that you will not be judged [for it]. Look! The Judge is standing right at the door."
> (James 5:9 AMP)

This verse of scripture is important to remember. I don't know about you, but I sure need some practice in not complaining, especially to my husband, and to God. Even when we feel justified – and at times we are justified – but we still need to not complain. When I complain to God in my prayer time, that spirit carries over into my conversation with my husband. Approaching my husband with this wrong stance or attitude sometimes gets me the results I want, but his agreement feels like a forced compliance, so the results don't last. And sweetheart, I have found that our husbands remember more about how we said something than the message we were trying to get across, especially when we are complaining and arguing. And they will begin to say all we do is complain, despite the fact that there were five days out of the week when we weren't complaining and only two days when we were. To them, the argument or conversation may as well have been taking place the whole week.

The Power of Praying Effectively

After my first few months of married life and praying amiss, I started feeling like God was speaking to my spirit saying He wanted to change *me*! I was surprised and a bit angry about that revelation, to say the least, but I began to look inwardly at which of my faults needed to change. I still have some moments when I pray like I did in those early months and years; however, now I know I must get my attitude right before God and pray more effectively if I want my prayers to be answered.

James confirms we must pray effectively, just seven verses down from the verse I quoted in the previous section:

"The effective, fervent prayer of a righteous man *(or woman)* avails much. (James 5:16 Words in italics added.)

The amplified translation says it this way:

"The heartfelt *and* persistent prayer of a righteous man (believer) can accomplish much [*when put into action and made effective by God—it is dynamic and can have tremendous power]. "* (James 5:16 AMP, emphasis added)

John chapter 5 says:

"Now this is the confidence that we have in **Him**, *that if we ask anything according to His will, He hears us*. And if we know that He hears us, whatever we ask, we know that we have the petitions that we have asked of Him." (1 John 5:14 – 15, emphasis added)

I have witnessed the power of effective, fervent, relentless prayer firsthand in my life. A family member once told me I had "bulldog" faith when it came to believing to have my children. I want to go back in time and tell you how God taught me about His faithfulness to answer if I will pray with all my heart and wait on Him.

Our Greatest Blessing from God

Gordon and I both wanted to have children. However, five years after our wedding day, I still had not gotten pregnant. As each month passed, I got more discouraged after I got my cycle. I can vividly remember rolling on the floor and crying out to God, "You can do anything that You want to do! I know You can bless me to get pregnant."

From the time I was a little girl, I had always wanted children. I wanted to have a son. The devil would harass me with thoughts that because I had gotten involved with drugs while I was in high school, I wouldn't ever be able to have children. The enemy would say, "Your womb is too polluted from all the drugs you've taken. You'll never be able to conceive a child."

One day, my sister-in-law gave me a book called *Supernatural Childbirth* by Jackie Mize. I cried all the way home that day because I didn't want to continue the cycle of getting my hopes up only to be let down again each month. I went straight to the chapter entitled "Confessions and Prayers" and started regularly praying the confession called "Before Pregnancy: Desire to Conceive, Fulfillment Over Barrenness."[2] I also read and meditated on the scriptures upon which the prayer was based. Soon, Gordon would join me in saying the prayer from the book.

Faith Without Action is Dead

One day, while standing inside the door to my boss's office, I announced, "I'm going to have a baby." I clarified that I was not pregnant yet, but I would be in time. Not too long after I made my declaration of faith to him, another co-worker, and Gordon (to whom I would say this phrase often), I got pregnant! Later on, I reflected back on how I didn't even realize what I was doing when I was speaking out what I was believing God would do. Jesus said that you will have what you say. And He would know best, as He was the Activator when God spoke the entire universe into existence! (See John 1:1-3.)

Not only did God bless me with one child, but I

also was blessed with a second child – both born in the same month less than three years apart! But God didn't stop there. He also blessed me with the handsome son that I had always wanted when I was a young girl!

So, I have seen the tremendous power of faith in action – praying fervently, having my church pray, and speaking God's word over my life. I mention these things because God was showing me the power which rests within His Word, and how faithful He is to bring His word to pass if I believe and trust Him. Not much later, after having my first child, I would benefit from this lesson of faith, so I could believe to keep my marriage vows.

The Power of a Word from God

While I was pregnant with my second daughter, Gordon came home from work early one evening and told me some unexpected news. He told me he had a son! His son had been born in Gordon's hometown before he and I had ever laid eyes on each other. Gordon had never said "I'm sorry" as much as he did that evening.

I was in shock. How, and more importantly, why did he take so long to tell me this? We had been married then for almost nine years! This was not a betrayal, but it felt like one. It was more like a deception – a serious omission of facts. And the thing that made it worse for me was Gordon was not even sitting me down to explain exactly what happened. I had many questions that were left unanswered!

The worse part for me was discovering that others had known when I didn't know. When I look back on this situation, it all connected back to a communication problem we had had for years, and the real reason for my unhappiness in my marriage. It felt like I was left out of the loop once again. It is difficult to be one with your spouse when secrets are kept from you.

In reflecting back now, I understand how others would have known about Gordon's son. However, back then, all I thought about was them knowing things I was not aware of, and being kept from this information made me feel like I wasn't part of the team. And really the "team" should have been Gordon and me first and foremost. I was totally in the dark about something that I should have been told up front. Later, I understood that my husband thought I would not marry him if he told me because I had made it clear to him that I didn't want any children by previous relationships. It was the "baby-mama drama" that I really didn't want, but nevertheless, this kind of thing really hurts when you are in the midst of it all.

Now here's the amazing part. When you are a child of God, He always has you covered. God had let me know that Gordon had a secret. I had a dream, and it was simply Gordon in it, and the feeling that he was not telling me something. That was God warning me about the situation. Another time, God let me know I was going to have a son. After that, I always thought I was going to give birth to a son, but God was speaking about my husband's son.

I will admit I spent the greater part of the following year rehashing this issue over and over again. My mother told me to stop talking about it. I mention it now because I thought of getting a divorce until I read Psalm 15. God communicated to me that I was to stick to my vows – the promises I made to my husband (and God) on that beautiful summer day in September 1990.

"Who may worship in your sanctuary, Lord? Who may enter your presence on your holy hill?... Those who lead blameless lives and do what is right, speaking the truth from sincere hearts. Those who refuse to gossip or harm their neighbors or speak evil of their friends. Those who despise flagrant sinners, and honor the faithful followers of the Lord, *and keep their promises even when it hurts.*" (Psalm 15: 1 – 4 NLT, emphasis added)

It was important to me to be obedient to what God was asking me to do. I've always had this type of mindset: I want to do God's will in my life, because I'm well aware that whatever He has in store will be much better than if I do things my way. We also will be held accountable for being disobedient to what God – through His Holy Spirit or through His word – has told us to do.

What do you sense the Holy Spirit has been instructing you to do concerning your marriage, and specifically, your marriage vows? If He has been telling you to do something, please try your best to obey His leading. I know it can be a difficult decision. But ask God to help you, and He will.

The Power of Forgiveness

Now I had the challenge of forgiving Gordon and then believing God could heal my heart as well as my marriage. I remember how God had to forgive me in the past – especially in my years as a young adult. So how could I dare not forgive Gordon or anyone else for that matter?

Is there anything you need to forgive your husband for? If so, take a few moments to pray about forgiving him. Write out anything that seems to keep you from doing so. Then, remove those hinderances of unforgiveness from your heart by writing "JESUS" across them with a red pen. Red will symbolize the blood of Jesus which allows us all to be forgiven. You can also write out a prayer of forgiveness here.

_____
_____
_____
_____
_____
_____

My Solution was in God's Word

After God led me to read Psalm 15, and my dad and my mother-in-law gave me sound advice, I knew I was supposed to stay married. I was going to need to exercise my faith once again. As I stated in chapter one, I had dreamed of being married since I was a little girl playing with my bride doll. I had met this good Christian man who had some flaws, but so did I, nevertheless, Gordan was a really great guy. I just needed to learn how to get through to him and get him to open his mouth and communicate with me. I too had my issues. Yes, I needed to pray, but very early on in my prayer sessions, God had already told me He wanted to do some work on me! So, I also needed to do some praying over myself! So, you see, I always knew God had a master plan for marriage, despite never seeing what His plan looked like. He created marriage, after all, so I had to do marriage His way!

At this point, having believed to have my children by praying God's word, I began to realize I was praying for my husband and my marriage incorrectly. I needed to pray the solution and not the problem. I found the solution for my marital problems in God's word.

This chapter began with Isaiah 55, verses 8 and 9 as a heading. The verses speak of how God's ways are entirely opposed to our ways of doing things (in the flesh). In the next two verses in chapter 55, God makes a profound analogy:

"The rain and snow come down from the heavens and stay on the ground to water the earth. They cause the grain to grow, producing seed for the farmer and bread for the hungry. It is the same with my word. I send it out, and it always produces fruit. It will accomplish all I want it to, and it will prosper everywhere I send it." (Isaiah 55: 9 – 10 NLT)

These verses tell us about the power and fruitfulness of the Word of God when He speaks it. Since we are created in God's image, you and I have the same ability to achieve a fruitful result in our lives when we declare God's promises over ourselves instead of speaking what we see in the present.

The Bible also clearly instructs us on the power of the words we speak out of our mouths. Proverbs says:

"Death and life *are* in the power of the tongue, and those who love it will eat its fruit." (Proverbs 18: 21)

How I Began Praying More Effectively

I have seen the power of praying God's word. I have also seen the power of agreeing in prayer when

Gordon and I prayed together, and I requested our church to pray for us. In the book of Matthew, Jesus taught about what happens when believers agree in prayer:

> "Again I say to you, that if two believers on earth agree [that is, are of one mind, in harmony] about anything that they ask [within the will of God], it will be done for them by My Father in heaven." (Matthew 18:19 AMP)

Even though you may not be able to get your husband to pray in agreement with you about the problems in your marriage, there will be some situations wherein you will need some prayer backup. Do your best to find a prayer group or someone else to agree with you in prayer. Choose wisely in whom you confide about your marriage. Choose women of God who are grounded in the word of God and who will honestly pray for your marriage or your husband and won't breach your confidence or try to use the information against you.

I have two such ladies in my life with whom I can share my issues. One lady is a dear friend who I've known since both of our children were in elementary school. She is a prayer warrior who goes to 5 AM prayer vigils with her children in tow. Also, my sister-in-law, who has been a prayer intercessor for over 30 years. These women I have confided in and asked them to pray for me, my husband Gordon, and my marriage. These ladies will pray with me at the drop of a hat, and will pray faithfully for me until I tell them the answer has been received!

In 1998, I bought *Prayers That Avail Much, Special Commemorative Gift Edition* by Germaine Copeland. This book has 156 scripture-based prayers, arranged and targeted to specific needs and groups of individuals. Some of my favorite prayers in this book are "Protection for Travel," "Compatibility in Marriage," "Harmonious Marriage," and "The Children," among others. [3]

After all of these years of praying God's word, I have noticed that I now have so much word in my spirit, I can write my own prayers. So, in addition to recommending the two books above, I have also written scripture-based prayers within the pages of this book.

Are You Doing Any Good for Your Husband?

In Proverbs, the Bible says that when a man finds a wife, he finds a good thing. I sometimes think about this verse when I am praying for my husband. What a marvelous blessing it is for a man to have a wife who prays for him! When you are taking the time to pray for your husband, you are truly doing him good. Men have lots of issues that they deal with on a daily basis, especially if your husband works and has a stressful or demanding job. There are many needs that he may have, that he may need you to pray about. Most of the time, he's not going to tell you, or even want to talk about them. Especially if they are job or business related. If that is the case, you can ask him if there's anything that you can pray about for him. He will usually answer yes if there is. Sometimes, you can just tell him, or send him a text letting him know, "I was praying for you today." You can also text him an encouraging scripture verse, or write it on a piece of paper and stick it in his jacket pocket, or just give it to him on a sticky note. I have written out scriptures for my husband to meditate on. It makes a difference in our husband's lives when we can be a blessing to them.

I started getting books that had scripture-based prayers for praying targeted prayers for my husband and my marriage. I purchased *The Power of a Praying Wife* by Stormie Omartian. This is a book consisting of 30 prayers – 29 for your husband, and 1 is for you the wife. Each scripture-based prayer has an accompanying chapter, and a list of the Bible verses contained in each prayer. My favorite prayers in this book are "His Protection," "His Health," "His Work," "His Affection," and "His Wife." [4] There are prayers as well which I highly recommend like "His Sexuality," "His Temptations," "His Finances," and "His Attitude."

I highly recommend the above book because of the author's candidness about marriage, the advice about the effectiveness of being a praying wife, and because the targeted areas are all there. Just look within the table of contents, find the chapter you need to read, and say the accompanying prayer over your husband. Since there are thirty prayers, you can get the book, and challenge yourself to say a prayer per day for an entire month. I employ a little different approach: I simply open it up – prayerfully asking God what I need to pray for my husband. And what it opens up to, I pray that prayer. If I have more time that day, I will read the accompanying chapter and highlight the parts that minister to me the most. The prayer for your husband's protection is a good one I try to pray often, along with the prayer for his health.

Below I have written some important things to pray about that will also help your marriage:

1. *You need to pray for yourself first.*
Spend time worshipping and praising God.
Ask God to give you a fresh anointing of the
Holy Spirit to see all of the good that is
inside of your husband – to focus on the
positive he does and remember exactly why
you fell in love with him in the first place.
Ask God to help you remember what it was
that you admired about your husband. What
turned you on about him? Ask God to give
you the love you once had for your husband.

2. *Thank God for your husband every
day.* If he's a good provider, thank God for
that. If he does something you really like,
thank God for that. Build your husband up
on his strengths as well. Come down from
that soap box of complaints and preaching
your sermons and adore your husband more.

3. *Pray daily for your husband*: his
health, his safety, and his work or business.
Psalm 91 is great to pray over your entire
family every day!

4. *Pray daily for your marriage.* Ask
God to heal anything that needs to be healed
in your marriage. Ask God to restore the
love, joy, and the fun back into your
marriage.

5. *Bind the devil away from your
marriage, your home, and yourself, your
husband, and your children each day.* Loose
the power of God, loose His mighty shield
of protection over your family, and plead the

shed blood of Jesus over your family as well.

    6.*Pray fervently for the things you see that are contrary to what God's word says should be according to His word.* Pray every day for your husband, using scripture- based prayers and your own personalized prayers. Pray targeted prayers for what he needs. The more specific the better. Go back and read Philippians 4:6-8 above.

    7.*Speak up for what is biblically right as the Holy Spirit leads you.* Also speak up for what you must have from your husband to keep your sanity and peace of mind. Do this in a completely respectful way and in a way that is non-threatening and will not belittle him.

Love your husband and do him only good all of the days of your life. (Proverbs 31:12) Praying for your husband every day is what will make a difference in his life and in your marriage. God will definitely meet you when you go to pray, and He will guide you along the way. He will reward your faithfulness to pray for your marriage. He will also speak to you directly about things that are of concern. Make time to worship, thank, and praise Him during your prayer time. You will not always have a lot of time to pray but make time each day. You can cover different areas or different people on different days. Let God lead you.

    "Dear Lord, Thank You for my husband. Help me to see him the way that You see him. I thank you for making me a wife, and for blessing me with the man that You chose for me. I thank You Lord, I asked You to send the husband that You had for me, and you sent me _____ (husband's name). Lord, you said that when a man finds a wife, he finds a good thing. Help me to be my husband's "good thing." Help me to love him and do him only good all the days of his life. Jesus, bless our marriage, bless our home, bless our finances, and increase the love we have for one another. Make us more in love than we ever have been! Help _____ (husband's name) and me to be more affectionate towards each other, to always greet each other with a kiss, and to talk freely with each other each day. Help me to desire only my husband sexually and help him to desire only me sexually.

Lord, show me how to build my husband up and not tear him down. The Bible says that a wise woman builds her house. Help me to build my house, and not tear it down like the foolish woman does. I ask You Lord for wisdom.

Lord, I bind anyone and anything away from our relationship, which would try to come against our union and the love that we share. Please get rid of any friendships, work situations, or family influences that are not conducive to our marriage being successful, happy, and strong. Take away from both of us any source of temptation to infidelity, indifference, or insecurity in our union.

Lord, only You know exactly what my husband's needs are within our marriage. But

Lord, I ask You to expose, remove, and reveal
whatever might be a hinderance to us staying
together and being extremely happy and content
with one another. Lord, help _____
(husband's name) to love me as Christ loves the
church. Help him to be kind, patient, loving,
thoughtful, and forgiving towards me, his
beloved wife. And help me to be respectful,
caring, thoughtful, tender, and forgiving of him,
my beloved husband.

Lord, help my husband to be (or continue
being) a rock-solid provider for our family.
Relieve some of the pressure and stress in his
life that may be work-related. Help my husband
to find godly outlets that will help him to relax
and enjoy his free time more.

If you have children:

Jesus, please help _____ to
(continue to) be a loving, patient, and dedicated
father and to spend quality time with our
children. Show him and teach him how to be a
father if it was not modeled properly when he
was growing up. Help me to plan getaways for
us to be alone, without the children, and to find
money to pay for it.

Most of all, Lord, help our home to be a
place of refuge, peace, joy, and laughter every
single day. Heal anything broken within our
marriage, Father. I give You every concern, and
every situation that needs fixing in it. Thank
You, Lord, for all of these blessings and more,
in Your Son Jesus Christ of Nazareth's name.
Amen."

I have written this prayer as a guide, or for you to pray exactly, on a daily basis. If you will pray for your husband, your marriage, and yourself, you will certainly see God answering your prayers. Remember, that you want to be consistent or persistent in your prayers for your husband and your marriage. Exercise your faith and wait on God to move in your marriage.

When I finished writing this prayer, I felt led to clean something that I had left unattended for a few months. I didn't understand why the Holy Spirit was seemingly leading me to clean at that exact moment. But after I was done, the Holy Spirit led me to go back and look at my work. When I did, I sensed Him saying, this is how I will clean up the marriage of the woman who will pray and ask me to clean up the problems she is facing in her marriage. Oh hallelujah! God is good.

Chapter Eight

What do You Mean, "Work on Me"?

Her husband… praises her, "Many daughters have done well, but you excel them all." Charm *is* deceitful and beauty *is* passing, but a woman *who* fears the Lord, she shall be praised. Give her of the fruit of her hands, and let her own works praise her in the gates. (Proverbs 31: 28b - 31)

The truth is that no one is going to change overnight. To expect that to happen would be unrealistic and unfair. Some things will take much longer than others, so what do you do while you're waiting for your husband to change? As I stated in chapter 7, God had let me know He wanted to change some things in *me*. I needed to work on me! Now, that doesn't mean just going off somewhere, and doing my own thing separate from my husband. However, what I am talking about is doing all the things I know I have always needed to do for myself, like focusing on taking better care of me—mentally emotionally, spiritually, vocationally, educationally, and physically. I had been too busy either fussing or focusing on what my husband and everybody else in the family was doing.

Dr. Harold J. Sala who pioneered the "Guidelines for Living" radio commentary heard around the world, and has been married for 60 years, gave some guidelines to follow when your mate needs to change:

> Guideline #1: "Stop trying to get your mate to change and love 'em "as is." Love begins where a person is. Understand that change is the result of God's Holy Spirit working in a person's life. There has to be a motive for change, and your being on someone's case isn't sufficient to affect long term personality changes."
>
> Dr. Sala's guideline #2: "*Strive to be the person God wants you to be. Much of the time we spend so much time and energy getting the other to change that we don't have time to concentrate on being the person we ought to be. Focus on being the right person, not making the other person right.*" ("3 Things To Do When Your Mate Needs To Change" www.guidelines.org, July 20, 2020)

God, or the Holy Spirit, is the best One to effectively make changes in our husbands. We won't ever be able to just program them to do something that we would prefer, as we would a robot or computer. And since this is the case, we may as well make better use of our time working on ourselves, working on getting more in touch with who God wants *us* to be, instead of always focusing on who we want our husbands to become.

I Had Forgotten the Strength Within Me

The challenge of becoming a wife is one in which you're trying to become "one" with your husband, and in the process, you may lose your own identity if you are not careful. So, one day, I realized God really wanted me to remember my strengths and let go of my weaknesses and fears.

I love the advice given to us wives in chapter 3 of 1 Peter, that follows:

> " Your adornment must not
> be *merely* external—with
> interweaving *and* elaborate knotting of the hair,
> and wearing gold jewelry, or [being
> superficially preoccupied with] dressing
> in *expensive* clothes; but let it be [the inner
> beauty of] the hidden person of the heart, with
> the imperishable quality *and unfading charm of
> a gentle and peaceful spirit, [one that is calm
> and self-controlled, not overanxious, but serene
> and spiritually mature]* which is very precious
> in the sight of God. For in this way in former
> times the holy women, who hoped in God, used
> to adorn themselves, being submissive to their
> own husbands and *adapting themselves to
> them; just as Sarah obeyed Abraham [following
> him and having regard for him as head of their
> house]*, calling him lord. **And you have become
> her daughters if you do what is right without
> being frightened by any fear [that is, being
> respectful toward your husband but not giving
> in to intimidation, nor allowing yourself to be
> led into sin, nor to be harmed]**." (1Peter 3: 3 –
> 6 AMP, emphasis added)

These verses are perhaps the capstone of what it

means to be a Christian wife. They speak of how we are to be submissive to our husbands, while also being spiritually whole – where inward beauty originates. And we are to be strong also, not being intimidated by, or fearful of our husbands. When we are not fearful of our husbands in a godly way, we possess an inner strength. This strength comes from times spent alone with God, in fellowship and prayer, and through studying His word.

I realized that I had allowed fear to take hold of me in my marriage. I had become fearful of speaking my mind to my husband. I had felt intimidated by him because of his reactions to my asking him questions about anything. He was often short-tempered and angry, and he would yell. I would remain calm because I wanted to remain respectful. Oftentimes, he would just leave the room abruptly and leave our home. I would always pray and give the situation to God while he was gone. Never staying very long, when he returned, there was never any further discussion or even a mention of the "argument" that had ensued. But this is not God's will for His daughters. Every time these problems arose and I prayed, God had seen it. Little did I know God wanted to make a change in me in order to help bring these incidents to an end.

God Wanted to Change Some Things in Me

If you begin to study the word and pray daily and earnestly for healing and direction, God will begin to show you things within yourself that you need to change. I realized this one day after an argument with my husband. Earlier that day, I had prayed as Gordon was driving and I was sitting in the silence that usually accompanied our rides in the car. I had grown tired of always having to start the conversations. And the silence always made me feel disconnected from him. So, I started typing out a prayer on the notepad app on my phone. I do this often as a way of communicating with God if I'm away from home and I'm not able to say my prayer out loud. I asked God to reveal to me what was at the root of Gordon's being so closed-mouthed and quiet with me, as this had been going on for years.

That evening, I got my answer. Gordon and I were relaxing in bed, and I thought I would bring up the problem of our communication. I said that maybe the reason we had difficulty connecting was that we both had been hurt before. Gordon immediately jumped in and began to remind me about something that happened within the first few years of our marriage. I had asked him if I could go to the funeral of an old boyfriend's mother. He said he'd told me no, but I said I was going anyway. When Gordon said I had told him no, I said that I was proud of myself – because at least I had had the courage to speak up for myself!

That's when he became really angry because I had said I was proud of myself. He went on to say that I had told him that this guy would always be a friend, and now I was saying that I was proud of myself.

I remember becoming so excited when Gordon told me my response to him. It was as though I was being re-introduced to the strong, opinionated, fearless young woman I had been before I got married and who I still was in my first five to ten years of marriage! Honestly, I had forgotten about her. Although, from time-to-time, I would reminisce about the young woman I used to be before I got married.

Although it wasn't right for me to go against what he told me to do, I explained that I was proud of myself for speaking up for what I had wanted to do. But Gordon was thinking about the part where I said this guy would always be a friend. He said this was when he had decided to hold back his communication from me.

Later on, after he had already left and I had prayed, he returned and went to the guest bedroom to sleep. I went in that room every 15 minutes, not letting him go to sleep. One of the times I swung the door open to tell him something, I told him this:

> "You know I'm sorry that I didn't do what
> you told me to do back then, but it's not like I
> was raised by my father, and I had practice with
> that sort of thing. I was raised by a single
> mother who made all of her own decisions. She
> didn't have anyone telling her what to do. (After
> some years, my mom did marry someone.)
> When my stepfather hit me, I didn't have one
> man in my family who I could call on to defend
> me. I only had a great-uncle, and he wasn't
> going to do anything. I called my dad, and he
> just came and got me and took me to his house.
> I'm sorry if I didn't do what you told me to do."

We ended up making up after I crawled into the guest bed with him. I told him the guy was nowhere close to the beautiful man he is (after all I had married him and not the other guy). We embraced and returned to our own bed. Later, we laughed about me busting into the room all those times and not allowing him to sleep.

I Didn't Need to Forget About Me

What I realized that night was God wanted me to remember who I am, where I have been, and to own the strength that was instilled in me from watching my strong mother, seeing how she overcame so many obstacles in life, and witnessing how she didn't let people walk all over her. I felt God's total acceptance of me—the way I am deep down inside—and He hadn't needed me to lose myself and who I am in order to fit in to someone else's idea of who I should become, even if that someone else was my own husband.

Also, God has not given us a spirit of fear that we should fear our husbands, being intimidated by them into silence and withdrawing into sadness and not enjoying our lives. (See 2 Timothy 1: 6 – 7 NLT.)

A wise young lady who had gone through a painful divorce told me, "The devil would like to silence us, so God's will won't be done in our lives."

Communicate With Confidence and Care

God had to show me that fear was not my story. Then I could effectively and confidently communicate with my husband. If you have suffered similar feelings as I have, this revelation will make a tremendous difference in your marriage. After you have prayed honestly and candidly to God about your most important needs being met in your marriage, and you have spoken God's word over your marriage, next have a serious talk with your husband about your needs not being met. Below, I am giving you some points for how you should communicate your concerns.

The Sandwich Technique. One of the reasons I had not been able to get my point across without making

Gordon so angry, and consequently he would just walk off or not want to even talk to me, was because I really did not realize the importance of the sandwich technique. When you are speaking to your husband about something you really need him to understand and hear from you, you have got to first give him some bread and put some butter on it. The bread is something you really have been needing to tell him—something very good that he does for you or for your family. But just like you wouldn't like a sandwich with a dry piece of bread, put some butter or at least some mayonnaise or mustard on it to help the meat (your problem) go down smoothly. The butter in your communication with your husband should be the sincere appreciation you have for him and all the great things he does. This is the caring part of your talk with your hubby.

Next, make him aware of the problem that's been occurring, and how it makes you feel. Give examples of the problem. Make analogies if needed. Make sure your meat is tasty so give what you want to say a lot of thought prior to sharing. This is when you will use confidence and precision to get your point across. Remember, most sandwiches are best served with just the right amount of meat. So be sure not to layer the problem on too thick.

Lastly, finish off with your second slice of bread. Tell him something else nice that he does, or something that will make him laugh or make you cry (because you genuinely care so much). Crying and you two laughing as well becomes the extra step of toasting your sandwich and making the bread nice and warm.

Pray God's Word Over You and Your Husband
When your needs aren't being met and you're not

happy, oftentimes you don't want to act nicely or be patient with your spouse. You are not in the mood to pray or confess God's word over your situation simply because you are tired of whatever is going on. You may feel like giving up. You want to tell God that you've done your best and you are done.

I know because I've been there. I literally had to get myself together and say the following confession with tears running down my face. Sometimes, you will need to say the confession below especially if you know you're going to have a very hard time being patient when you talk to your husband about your unmet needs. Maybe you have already been telling him about it and you may have come across with a little too much power or force. Speaking the scriptures in this confession will make you feel immediately strengthened, and give you an opportunity to take authority over your marriage problem in the spirit realm!

> "Father, in the name of Jesus, the love of God is shed abroad in our hearts by the Holy Spirit Who indwells us. Therefore, my spouse and I are learning to endure long and are patient and kind; we are never envious and never boil over with jealousy. We are not boastful or vainglorious, and we do not display ourselves haughtily. We are not conceited or arrogant and inflated with pride. We are not rude and unmannerly, and we do not act unbecomingly. We do not insist on our own rights or our own way, for we are not self-seeking or touchy or fretful or resentful. We take no account of the

evil done to us and pay no attention to a suffered wrong. We do not rejoice at injustice and unrighteousness, but we rejoice when right and truth prevail.

We bear up under anything and everything that comes. We are ever ready to believe the best of each other. Our hopes are fadeless under all circumstances. We endure everything without weakening. Our love never fails — it never fades out or becomes obsolete or comes to an end.

We are no longer children tossed to and fro, carried about with every wind of doctrine, but we speak the truth in love, dealing truly and living truly. We are enfolded in love, growing up in every way and in all things. We esteem and delight in one another, forgiving one another readily and freely as God in Christ has forgiven us. We are imitators of God and copy His example as well-beloved children imitate their father.

Thank You, Father, that our marriage grows stronger each day because it is founded on Your Word and on Your kind of love. We give You the praise for it all, Father, in the name of Jesus. Amen." (Compatibility in Marriage, www.prayers.org/compatibilityinmarriage, March 5, 2017)

When you speak God's word, you are activating angels, as it says in Psalm 103, verse 20.

Let's Do the Work

It is vitally important that we spend some time

working on ourselves. Figure out exactly what floats our boat, what we need from our husbands, and why we need it. Concentrate not only on what we need from our spouses, but also focus on what we need from ourselves as well. Communication is key, but how we communicate with our husbands is also important. We should not allow our husbands to ignore our needs, silence our voices, or take our power away. We have to spend some time in God's presence first and build ourselves up in prayer. This is accomplished by praying in the spirit and with understanding, and asking God for both wisdom and strength.

We have to make a routine of regularly spending time alone with God on our knees. As we spend time with God, He will reveal who we really are and the "us" that He wants us to get back in touch with, as well as become. Finally, reading God's word is an essential part of this process of working on ourselves because this is one of the ways God will reveal Himself to us.

Also, take authority over your health and your wealth. Ask God for direction. God wants to heal every aspect of your being. As you feel more whole within yourself, you will be able to realize the necessary changes you must make first. Then what you need from your spouse will come as you pray, wait on God, get your joy back. God will help you to set a new standard for what you allow to take place in your interaction. You will not permit anyone to steal your joy.

TANIA CHAPMAN SCOTT

Chapter Nine
But I Want the Divorce Possibility

For the Lord, the God of Israel, says: I hate divorce *and* marital separation and him who covers his garment [his wife] with violence. Therefore, keep a watch upon your spirit [that it may be controlled by My Spirit], that you deal not treacherously *and* faithlessly [with your marriage mate]. Malachi 2:16 (AMPC)

Despite the prevalence and wide acceptance of divorce in our culture today and even within the Church, this was not God's original plan for marriage. When God created marriage, He intended for the couple to remain married and not divorce. This is a difficult point to sell, especially in today's culture and mindset. Today, some people get married and divorced like they change hairstyles or upgrade to a new model and year automobile. Even within the church, divorce has become almost a norm due to the frequency of occurrence within Christian marriages. And with the internet being just a finger's reach away, divorce websites are everywhere, and dissatisfied spouses can easily search ways to quickly end their marriages.

According to statistics on itsovereasy.com, a divorce attorney's website for online divorce, "When divorced people are surveyed about what caused their marriage to end, 73% cite lack of commitment as a contributing factor." This appears to say that someone simply got up one day and decided, "I'm done, I don't feel like being married anymore." As a friend said to me recently, "We don't fight for our marriages." This means people are just giving up instead of fighting to keep their marriage strong and successful. As an African American myself, the following statistic really hits home: based on surveys conducted in 2020, the rate of divorce for Black couples was the second highest (behind Native Americans) with 42% of both Black men and women experiencing at least one divorce.

Even though the divorce rate in America declined according to the U.S. Census Bureau from 2009 to 2019, the U.S. still had the sixth highest rate of divorce in the world – with 40 to 50 percent of married couples filing for a divorce. In 2020, the national average for divorce was 2.3 per 1,000 people (down from 2.7 per 1,000 people in 2019), as the Centers for Disease Control reported. And though there was a slight decline, the number of divorces was 630,505 in 2020 alone. ("48 Divorce Statistics in the U.S. Including Divorce Rate, Race, & Marriage Length," divorce.com, updated October 28, 2022.)

Since the above-mentioned statistics apply to the general population in the U.S., let's look at how Christians in particular did in the area of divorce? In 2008, "the Barna Group calculated that for every three married adult Born Again Christians, at least one of them was divorced, making the rate among married Born Again Christian adults about 33 percent." But there were some subsequent studies which revealed that, of the Christian group who divorced in the original findings, 38 percent of them attended church weekly. And 60 percent of that original group of divorced couples affiliated with being Christian but did not attend church on a weekly basis.

The finding that 60 percent of the divorced Christians did not regularly attend church, is perhaps confirmation of the truth in Hebrews, chapter 10, where it tells us not to forsake the assembling of ourselves together with fellow Christians:

> "Not forsaking *or* neglecting to assemble together [as believers], as is the habit of some people, but admonishing (warning, urging, and encouraging) one another, and all the more faithfully as you see the day approaching." (Hebrews 10: 25 AMPC)

If, in God's word, Christians are reminded not to forget to come together with other believers in fellowship to worship God and receive instruction, then God knew that there would be a benefit in His children doing that. We should definitely walk in obedience to this command. At our church, Gordon and I have met other couples with whom we enjoy fellowshipping, and with whom we have gone out to dinner on occasion. Our church also has couples' groups, and we have a strong focus on Bible-based teaching. Still, it is up to each person attending our church to study the Bible on our own, not only by attending church weekly on Sunday, but also by going to mid-week studies where oftentimes the message from Sunday is studied further. And with 60% of the divorced Christians not attending church on a weekly basis, it seems obvious that lack of concentration on God's word is most likely a huge contributing factor to failed marriages.

As I stated in chapter 2, the devil likes to attack marriages, especially Christian ones, so we need to put on the whole armor of God and be ready for his attacks, do battle, resist him, and not give place to him in our homes (Ephesians 4:27). We also need to be very selective about the couples or individuals we befriend, even within the church. There have been many an affair that has occurred between churchgoing Christians. Even some pastors and pastor's wives have been caught up in infidelity with someone else's husband or wife! The devil is like a roaring lion, going around seeking who he may devour. Therefore, let us be sober, vigilant (cautious) of who we allow within our marital circle. (See 1 Peter 5: 8.)

I could go on and on about citing the statistics of divorce within our society. However, divorce is not what God had in mind for our marriages. You can only imagine that since God's will in the beginning was that the man and his wife would become one flesh, that it was not His original intent that so many would be following their own wills and getting divorces. It also seems as though many of these divorces are taking place without so much as a prayer to even ask God to help or without even wondering if the split is His will.

Once again, I am not here to tell anyone you should stay with someone who is being physically or even emotionally abusive toward you. But even if your husband cheated on you—which is a biblically justified reason to divorce—I would recommend that you still pray and ask for God's direction. If for nothing else but to help ease the pain and the hurt of it all.

In Matthew chapter 19, Jesus said that what God has joined together, no one should separate. Listen to what He told the Pharisees after they asked him a question about divorce. They were trying to get him to say something contrary to their man-made-up rules and policies. But as usual, Jesus shows them He is quite aware of what was stated in what we now call the Old Testament. This is the account of what Jesus said to them:

> "When Jesus had completed these teachings, he left Galilee and crossed the region of Judea on the other side of the Jordan. Great crowds followed him there, and he healed them. One day the Pharisees were badgering him, "Is it legal for a man to divorce his wife for any reason?" He answered, "Haven't you read in your Bible that the Creator originally made man and woman for each other, male and female? And because of this, a man leaves father and mother and is firmly bonded to his wife, becoming one flesh—no longer two bodies but one. Because God created this organic union of the two sexes, no one should desecrate his art by cutting them apart." They shot back in rebuttal, "If that's so, why did Moses give instructions for divorce papers and divorce procedures?" Jesus said, "Moses provided for divorce as a concession to your hard heartedness, but it is not part of God's original plan. I'm holding you to the

original plan, and holding you liable for adultery if you divorce your faithful wife and then marry someone else. I make an exception in cases where the spouse has committed adultery." Jesus' disciples objected, "If those are the terms of marriage, we haven't got a chance. Why get married?" But Jesus said, "Not everyone is mature enough to live a married life. It requires a certain aptitude and grace. Marriage isn't for everyone. Some, from birth seemingly, never give marriage a thought. Others never get asked—or accepted. And some decide not to get married for kingdom reasons. But if you're capable of growing into the largeness of marriage, do it."" (Matthew 19: 1 – 12 MSG)

Why do you think Jesus said "not everyone is mature enough to live a married life. It requires a certain aptitude and grace"? Do you feel like you have the maturity to which He was referring or not? If not, what do you think might help you raise yourself to a higher level of maturity with God so you may be able to have a successful marriage and avoid divorce?

_____
_____
_____
_____
_____
_____
_____
_____

_____

_____

_____

_____

_____

I was praying one day when God gave me this statement. And, as I have recently started a habit of doing, I wrote it on an index card:

> "You and your husband have been made one when you stood before God on your wedding day. How can this be undone without an incredible amount of pain and suffering?"

There are many side effects of divorce. Let's start with some of the effects divorce can have on children.

> "According to the National Library of Medicine, more than one million children in the United States experience their parents' divorce each year. In addition, only 60 percent of children in the U.S. live with their married, biological parents, and these vast numbers make the effects of divorce on children a matter of public health.

> **Psychological Effects of Divorce on Children**

> Studies from the National Library of Medicine have found that divorce can negatively impact a child's mental health and overall well-being. This is due to a number of reasons, including feelings of instability and lack of support while their parents are going through a divorce. It's important to remember that most children will not experience short- and

long-term effects of divorce, but negative effects are possible. Some psychological effects of divorce on children include:
•Increased academic difficulties, including lower grades and higher rates of school dropout
•Disruptive behaviors, such as delinquency or substance use
•Increased rates of depression and other mental illnesses
•Higher risk of developing Chronic Daily Headaches (CDH)
•Increased risk of developing lifetime Attention Deficit Hyperactivity Disorder (ADHD)
•More likely to develop an eating disorder
•Increased risk of developing an anxiety disorder" ("Effects of Divorce on Children and How to Help Them Through It," divorce.lovetoknow.com, Aubrey Freitas, updated May 25, 2022)

Now, let's move on to some of divorce's effects on the wife:

"The Effects of Divorce on Women: Most divorced couples expect to go through a tough adjustment period immediately after the marriage comes to an official end. It's important to be aware of the possible consequences of divorce, and to have a realistic view of the future. Only in movies does a rich, handsome, eligible man appear out of nowhere and give a divorced woman everything she has ever dreamed of and more. In real life, women normally suffer the most after a divorce, both in terms of quality of life and emotional well-being, says Michele Weiner Davis, creator of the Divorce Busting Centers.

Financial Distress: The average divorced woman has less money than the average married woman and women don't completely recover from the financial consequences of divorce until they remarry,

Emotional Distress: Divorced women reported significantly higher psychological distress levels than married women in the years following the divorce. The stresses of being in an unhappy marriage may simply be replaced by different worries, such as not being able to trust a man again, struggling to find her perfect partner or a fear of being rejected.

Freedom: Despite the potential negative effects of divorce on a woman, there are many cases in which divorce leads to a happier, healthier life. If a woman is getting out of a marriage fraught with conflict or violence she will be happier in the long term. A woman may still require professional help.

Taking Control: For a divorce to have more positive effects on a woman than negative, she must make the most of the chance to change her life for the better. Some women say that the first few years after divorce are a time of significant personal growth, with greater independence and more personal choices. It is crucial to work to create a better life, ..." ("The Effects of Divorce on Women," oureverydaylife.com, C. Giles, updated on December 5, 2018)

As I stated in chapter six, some women want a divorce, thinking they will be happier with someone else, but statistics tell us that second and third marriages have lower chances of success than first marriages. First, I have come to realize it's a risky proposition to think someone else is going to do a better job of meeting your needs than your current spouse. How do you know what you will be getting in the new man? Will he be a better match for you? Will he start out treating you wonderfully, being all that you imagined you ever wanted in a husband, and then after a year or two of marriage, you end up realizing you have married a bonafide idiot who is criminally abusive and not at all what you imagined? I mean, it could all work out and you end up being the happiest you've ever been, but the statistics do not support this positive outcome.

The diagram below illustrates the chances of divorce for first marriages, second marriages, and third marriages:

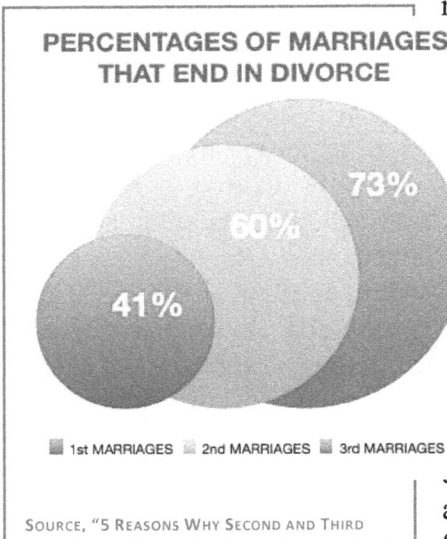

PERCENTAGES OF MARRIAGES THAT END IN DIVORCE

73%

60%

41%

1st MARRIAGES 2nd MARRIAGES 3rd MARRIAGES

SOURCE, "5 REASONS WHY SECOND AND THIRD

In looking at the numbers, there are slight variations, depending on the source. However, the general rule I saw was, while divorces first marriages are implicated from 40 to percent, the rates divorce in second and third marriages are much higher. Second marriage divorce rates are reported from 60 – 68 percent, and third marriage divorce rates are stated right around 73 or 74 percent. Now, what are the reasons for these statistics? One article online said this:

> "If someone has been through a divorce once before, and knows they can make it through this tragic, life-altering ordeal, then maybe they are less terrified of going through it again when the (stuff) hits the fan. The thought process might be "I've done it once, lived to tell the tale, and can survive it....again." They may also be more inclined to run at the first sign of trouble. So, it's not that one gets better at marriage with every marriage, it's that one gets better at divorce with every marriage." ("9 Reasons Why Second (and Third) Marriages Are More Prone to Divorce," survivedivorce.com, Nicole Smith, n.d.)

The abovementioned article also cites other reasons such as baggage from previous marriages, getting married too quickly (another article referred to it as trying to heal from the first marriage by way of the second marriage), no children to stay married for, difficulties of having a blended family, and money issues associated with having to pay exes' support. Another reason that was mentioned for the high divorce rates in subsequent divorces was being in denial about the role you played in the failure of the previous marriage.

Since second and third marriages have lower chances of success than first marriages, I challenge you to get clear on not only why you may want a divorce, but also to look down the road and consider all the possible ramifications of doing so. I have not personally gone through a divorce. However, as I mentioned earlier, I have thought about getting one and I might have very well gone through with it, had it not been for God intervening and also my heeding some very good advice from family members.

I doubt that I would have taken the time to research information about the aftermath of divorce, prior to going ahead with it. Most people probably research what the process is to file the divorce and later on deal with the fallout of taking that step. The whole purpose of me writing this book is so that any wife reading it can have an opportunity to really think about pursuing another way of looking at her marriage and try to avoid divorcing. Therefore, unless you have very valid and biblical justification for it, I highly recommend that you give your marriage your best effort to make it work. (I am so happy that you are reading this book and I have been so blessed as well having written it!)

Scriptures to Wives About Divorce

Most scriptures are directed to men who want to divorce their wives; however, the Bible does speak directly to women who want to divorce their husbands. Below are two scriptures which pertain to wives divorcing their husbands:

> "But to the married people I give charge—
> not I but the Lord—that the wife is not to
> separate from her husband. But if she does
> [separate from and divorce him], let her remain
> single or else be reconciled to her husband. And
> [I charge] the husband [also] that he should not
> put away *or* divorce his wife. To the rest I
> declare—I, not the Lord [for Jesus did not
> discuss this]—… if any woman has an

unbelieving husband and he consents to live with her, she should not leave *or* divorce him. For the unbelieving husband is set apart (separated, withdrawn from heathen contamination, and affiliated with the Christian people) by union with his consecrated (set-apart) wife, and the unbelieving wife is set apart *and* separated through union with her consecrated husband. Otherwise, your children would be unclean (unblessed heathen, outside the Christian covenant), but as it is they are prepared for God [pure and clean]." (1 Corinthians 7: 10 – 12a, 13 – 14 AMPC)

"And He said to them, Whoever dismisses (repudiates and divorces) his wife and marries another commits adultery against her; *and if a woman dismisses (repudiates and divorces) her husband and marries another, she commits adultery.*" (Mark 10: 11 – 12 AMPC, emphasis added)

Women Initiating Divorce

In a 2015 Annual Meeting of the American Sociological Association, Michael Rosenfeld, a professor of sociology at Stanford University, presented his findings that women initiate 69% of all divorces. So why do women initiate the split in two-thirds of all divorces? In an article on divorcemag.com, Julie Danielson, a Women's Empowerment Coach, had the following to say on this subject:

"Usually, when a woman comes to me, they have already decided to divorce. But there are times that I wonder if that divorce was necessary, or was it just easier? … Women seek closeness and vulnerability in a marriage where, under the veil of marriage, it is safe to be real and raw with our chosen one, or soul mate. When she reaches out for that connected feeling and is met with the "wrong" response, she lays a brick down. Then one day, the wall is too high to penetrate it. In its simplest form, deep down, women crave connection with their partners – but many women have the erroneous belief that if their husbands *really* loved them, they would instinctively *know* what their wives wanted, so a man needs to be a proficient mind-reader to know how to satisfy their wife's need for connection. This is where the communication breakdown often occurs: women not saying what it is they want ("If he truly loved me, he'd already *know* what I want!"), and men not "getting it" ("I can't do *anything* right as far as she's concerned, so I might as well stop trying!") So, resentment festers and the walls go up."

("The Breaking Point: Why Do Women Initiate Divorce More Than Men?," Julie Danielson, divorcemag.com, updated July 21, 2022)

As Ms. Danielson stated, and I said in the last chapter, it is important for us wives to communicate what our most important needs are in the relationship. (Remember to pick your battles – not everything can be our way!) We must be forthright about the changes we need so we can feel valued and respected. Often, these conversations do not need to be some long drawn-out speeches or tongue lashings. Your husband may not respond favorably initially. He may not even respond at all. He may not take you seriously or make any changes initially. However, letting your husband know how you must be treated, is well worth you achieving a higher level of happiness, joy, peace, and a more successful marriage.

Speaking up can help you avoid a needless divorce as well. Always walk in forgiveness, pray, talk to God daily about your marriage, and surrender to His will. At the end of the day, it is only God Who has the ability to hold your marriage together and make it a masterpiece. He will hold your marriage together the same way in which He holds the universe together!

When it comes to the point where you are considering or thinking about divorce, it seems that your focus is heavily on all the things your husband does wrong. It's difficult not to focus on the hurtful things. After all, he gives you a lot of negative behaviors to look at. But this is when the devil is able to do his strategic work of getting you to hone in on that one thing—or perhaps a multitude of events—that hurt you so much. It could be how he is always being pulled away from spending quality time with you because of work, family, or friends. Or maybe it's his lack of showing you the attention or focus you so desperately need and want from your man. He leaves you feeling taken for granted and like your years are being wasted.

But what you don't see during these moments—or you fail to remember—are the little things he's done along the way to demonstrate his love. Have you considered some of the following:

He comes home after work. Some men don't come home until really late, or not at all.

He watches your favorite television show with you. Some men only watch sports or are just always on their phones twenty-four/seven.

He was there with you when your children were born.

He stayed with you in the emergency room when you got sick. Some husbands seem to not care.

He gets up faithfully every darn day to go to work to take care of paying the bills. Some men just lay around and want their wives to do all the work inside and outside of the home!

I'm not saying you must settle for just these things, but I am asking you to consider that just maybe things in your marriage could be a lot worse.

Do a little scavenger hunt around your house. I ended up doing this quite by accident because I was putting away a few items after having some work done in our home. In the process, I found many little trinkets and memorabilia that reminded me of the little things I made mention of above—the little things we forget about when we are focusing on everything our husbands do that make us unhappy.

Take five to ten minutes and look around your home. Look on your living room table and in the kitchen junk drawer. Look at the photos on the wall or on your phone's photo app. Look for something that might remind you of some time that you and your husband did something fun together, he did something sweet or unexpected, etc. Did you find anything? If not yet, over the course of the next few days, keep a look out.

Even if you don't find anything in your home to remind you of happier times or times when your husband was thoughtful, know that God says, "Vengeance is Mine, I shall repay." God, being the omnipresent God that He is, sees everything our husbands do, including everything we do as well. If your husband is being unfair about something or not treating you in accordance with God's Word, then your husband will have to answer to God for that.

In writing this chapter, I have tried to give you some things to think about. You may not have even been seriously thinking about divorce. But if you ever do, I want you to come back and read this chapter. You never know when the devil might try to come to your mind with some mess to try to sabotage your marriage. We bind him in the name of Jesus! Amen.

TANIA CHAPMAN SCOTT

Chapter Ten

Just Tell Me the One Thing That Will Truly Change My Marriage

And the effect of righteousness will be peace, and the result of righteousness, quietness and trust forever. My people will abide in a peaceful habitation, in secure dwellings, and in quiet resting places. (Isaiah 32: 17 – 18 ESV)
Choose to Live in Peace with Your Spouse

One of the best things you can do for yourself and your marriage is to commit to live in peace with your mate. As I have already stated, sex in marriage is a husband's number one need, other than respect and companionship. But what good is sex and respect to your husband, if there is no peace in your home? This is why so many husbands would actually choose peace in their marriage over having sex if given a choice between the two.[1] How do you achieve a state of peace with your husband?

It's Alive!

Your marriage is a living and breathing creation. It's alive even though it may seem like it's dead at times. Your marriage is a real living organism! God created it when you said those vows to which you really may not have given much thought. When you said your vows to your husband on your wedding day, guess who heard every word? God did. He wrote down your spouse's and your name. Of course, God didn't need to actually write down your names because he knew just who you would marry even before you met.

I mention that your marriage is alive because you must feed it. Give it water, attention, good thoughts, and prayers. In this chapter, I want you to focus on the importance of filling your heart with the good things that God has to offer your marriage, instead of the lies and tricks of the enemy who will try to end it. Why is filling your heart with good things so important? Because the way you think about your marriage, or your mindset, will definitely affect the success or failure of it.

Chapter 4 of Philippians tells us to always think the best of others and to think on whatever is good. This is more than good advice; it's really a commandment from God, Who inspired the Apostle Paul, by His Holy Spirit, to write it:

> "Always be full of joy in the Lord. I say it again—rejoice! Let everyone see that you are considerate in all you do. Remember, the Lord is coming soon. Don't worry about anything; *instead, pray about everything. Tell God what you need and thank him for all he has done.* Then you will experience God's peace, *which exceeds anything we can understand. His peace will guard your hearts and minds as you live in Christ Jesus.* And now, dear brothers and

sisters, one final thing. **Fix your thoughts on what is true, and honorable, and right, and pure, and lovely, and admirable. Think about things that are excellent and worthy of praise.** Keep putting into practice all you learned and received from me—everything you heard from me and saw me doing. **Then the God of peace will be with you.**" (Philippians 4: 4 – 9 NLT, emphasis added)

In the last two chapters, I wrote about the importance of communicating with your husband about your greatest needs. But do this along with prayer and thinking the best thoughts of your husband and your marriage. This will bring you peace, joy, and fulfillment of God's plan in your marriage relationship. You see, they all work together! You cannot *just* communicate what you need from your husband without praying over what you say before and after. Nor can you *just* think good thoughts. You also cannot pray without staying positive, forgiving your husband, and thanking God for the good you're believing Him to do in your marriage! These components are all necessary pieces that God somehow fits together into one neat package called "your marriage restoration plan."

Trust in God
You can't go wrong by putting all of your trust in God. He's the one who will never let you down. That's the only way we are going to keep our peace in the midst of walking through this journey called life. The book of Isaiah speaks of another way to maintain your peace. It says that those who keep their minds focused

on God will be kept in complete and absolute peace because they know in Whom they trust.

> "You will keep *him* in perfect peace,
> *Whose* mind *is* stayed *on You,* because he trusts in You." (Isaiah 26: 3)

So, it is important also to trust God, after you have prayed, kept your thoughts focused on the good, and communicated your greatest needs. An excellent way to keep your mind focused on the good and on God, is by seeking it and Him within His word. Keep a Bible app on your phone. Read the highlighted scripture for the day. Read a proverb a day, as there are 31 proverbs, you can read the chapter of proverbs for that day's date. You can do the same thing with a chapter from Matthew, however this book has only 28 chapters, so the last two or three days you would need to get creative.

I was feeling really down about my marriage one day. I went to the nail salon for some me time, but I still felt down. I then typed a quick prayer out on my phone's notes app. No change—there still remained this feeling of sadness. Then I noticed some notes I had taken during a message at my church in May of 2019:

> "If my hope is in the written Word of God, then I will not be disappointed…" ("Prescription For A Healthy Life", Pastor Kenneth Mulkey, Cottonwood Church, May 5, 2019)

After I read this, I immediately opened my Bible app and read the Verse of the Day. It was Galatians 6:7-

8. Then I kept reading through verse 9 and the whole passage says:

> "Do not be deceived, God is not mocked; for whatever a man sows, that he will also reap. For he who sows to his flesh will of the flesh reap corruption, but he who sows to the Spirit will of the Spirit reap everlasting life. And let us not grow weary while doing good, for in due season we shall reap if we do not lose heart." (Galatians 6: 6 – 9)

All that day, I had been feeling down. I had been feeling sorry for myself, and secular music droned from the radio in my car. The music was fun for some time, but after a while I had to change the station because the songs were not what I needed to be hearing. I had even been saying some bad things that day. I had good reason to feel down, but I had been "sowing to my flesh" that day, and not "sowing to the Spirit." Seeing Pastor Ken's words in my notes, and then reading those verses on my Bible app really helped me get my mind focused back on the things of the Spirit so I could reap the things of the Spirit. We need to stay focused on the good things of God and how we will reap the benefits of our faithfulness if we do not faint or give up.

Maintain Your Peace at All Times

Whatever you do, don't let your husband's ways, moods, or mistakes ruin your peace. I would definitely have to admit that one of my biggest struggles in my marriage and in my life has been letting others disturb my peace. I am a happy person by nature. With the exception of those days when I haven't had a good night's rest, I usually start each new day in my own space of joy, peace, and thankfulness. However, if someone does something or says something off putting, I would usually let this spoil my mood.

One day while signing in to start work, all of a sudden, the office manager said something to me. I got upset and had words with her. Right there in the middle of the main office, there I was shouting something back to her. Just that quickly, I had allowed someone who usually had a dry attitude anyway, affect the beginning of my day.

It has been a similar thing with my marriage, but instead of me ending up shouting and angry at Gordon, I would be sad and depressed because of him changing moods on me. For years, if not decades, I allowed this to take away the joy I woke up with that morning. Finally, I declared, "Enough is enough. I am not going to continue to allow other people to change who I am at my core."

A person's peace is a gift from God. Jesus said He left us peace when He ascended on high to rejoin the Father in heaven. He said the following in the fourteenth chapter of John:

> "I am leaving you with a gift—peace of mind and heart. And the peace I give is a gift the world cannot give. So don't be troubled or afraid." (John 14: 27 NLT)

Life is too short to allow others to cause you to spend it being upset, living in sadness, or feeling depressed. Today, I'm making it a priority to pray over my marriage and over myself proactively on a daily basis, and then reactively when needed. I am starting to see that sometimes I need to speak with my actions more so than with my words. I need to move on with my life, doing the things I need to get done instead of spending so much energy on what my husband may not be doing.

Also, I am starting to make time to do the things I love doing—things that bring me peace and joy. I do not have control over my husband's mood, or anyone else's mood for that matter, but I do have control over my mood and my reaction to others.

Some time ago, I heard the phrase in my spirit, "Withdraw emotionally," after my husband had changed his mood. I had already said a one sentence response to him, and then I told him I was going for a walk. Initially, I hadn't planned on going too far, but I went "all the way around" – a 3 ½ mile walk – basically because I was mad. I had such a wonderful time, and I reminded myself how much I enjoy getting out in nature and walking, since I had not walked that far for several months. I returned home, went upstairs, and started reading my Bible and taking notes. When I looked up, there Gordon was, asking me if I was busy. That was his way of making up with me, and God had shown me how to handle his mood swings.

I am growing now. I am being led by the Spirit more, and I am trusting God to show me things. Right now, I'm learning how to just be content with myself and be happy regardless of what is going on around me. This is something I have needed to learn how to do since I was in my twenties. I'm starting to learn how to live my best life as they say. Withdrawing emotionally doesn't mean you withdraw from being your husband's wife and from being his help mate.

If your husband is yelling, being disrespectful, whatever the case may be, pray about it. Let him know it's not acceptable and give him to God! Also, tell God you cannot put up with that treatment any longer. Ask Him to do something about it, because you know that it is not His will for you to live in such conditions.

Learn to Like Your Husband Again and Meet His Needs While You're at It!

Learn to like your husband again. Endeavor to understand his needs and try your best to meet them. Have you ever found yourself saying within your head (and hopefully not out loud), "I hate you," or "I can't stand you," or "I really don't like you"? Well, if you have, don't worry because we all have had our moments of sinful thoughts. Know that this is not God's will for how we should be feeling about our husbands. I had to repent of saying one of these phrases after I ended up getting sick one time.

I hadn't gotten a good night's rest. Things happened. I got angry at my husband and ended up saying "I hate you" in my head. The interesting thing was that later, Gordon told me he was aware I felt that way. Even if we don't say things out loud, those closest to us can pick up on our negative emotions.

You want to be ever so careful about harboring bad feelings towards your husband because then you can be giving place to the devil. The devil would love for you to be walking around saying you hate your husband. And that's when you can open yourself up to every evil thing and not have God's covering if you don't repent quickly. Most likely, when you get to this point, you have not been reading God's word or praying. The Bible says if we have unconfessed sin—iniquity—in our hearts, God cannot hear our prayers:

"If I had not confessed the sin in my heart, the Lord would not have listened." (Psalm 66:18 NLT)

We want to repent of harboring any sin in our hearts and learn to like our husbands, love them, and enjoy spending time with them. We want to do the things that make them feel loved, cared for, and special. If we don't, believe me, somebody else will.

You might say, "Okay, that's fine. Good luck to her!" But I don't know about you, but I will be darned if there will be any Christmas cards coming in the mail with my husband's and some other woman's name on them. I bind that, in the name of Jesus! I love my husband. And I am going to keep him satisfied!

So, pay attention to what your husband has told you he likes. You can ask him if you're not sure, then get busy making time to do some of those things each week—or better yet—each day to please your husband! You can still do these things in the midst of telling him what you need to have from him. In fact, that makes him more likely to be in a better mood and listen to what you have to say.

Live Free from Unforgiveness and Negative Emotions

I know. Living free from unforgiveness and negative emotions can sometimes be easier said than done. If your husband has a difficult personality or is prone to moodiness, it can be a real challenge to want to forgive him. Oftentimes, I just need an attitude adjustment after experiencing some of that from my husband! I would rather deal with him another way than allowing the devil to steal my joy. You might wonder where the devil comes in. You may ask, "Didn't you say it was your husband being difficult or moody?" Yes, I said the devil. The Bible tells us we wrestle not with flesh and blood, but with principalities and rulers of wickedness in high places. It's the devil who wants to have your underwear all in a bunch and have you fighting with your husband.

When I start feeling a little like "I just want to get away," that's when I get quiet and focus on me. I run some bath water, go get a pedicure, or go shopping for something I have been wanting or needing. I may just do all of the above. One of the greatest things you can do for yourself is to be as independent as possible. Seek God for wisdom and guidance about your career and having an income of your own. Study Proverbs 31:10 – 31 if you haven't already. Save some money each paycheck for when you want to do something nice for yourself. You can do something as small as going to your favorite store and getting some skincare item, a workout outfit for the gym, or a cute pair of earrings that you love. Play some good worship music on your way to the store. Praise and worship helps me to get a mindset modification. Colossians chapter 3 says:

> "Set your mind on things above, not on things on the earth. For you died, and your life is hidden with Christ in God. When Christ *who is* our life appears, then you also will appear with Him in glory… But now *you yourselves are to put off all these: anger, wrath, malice, blasphemy, filthy language out of your mouth*…Therefore, as *the* elect of God, holy and

beloved, *put on tender mercies, kindness, humility, meekness, longsuffering; bearing with one another, and forgiving one another, if anyone has a complaint against another; even as Christ forgave you, so you also must do.* But *above all these things put on love,* which is the bond of perfection. **And let the peace of God rule in your hearts, to which also you were called in one body; and be thankful. Let the word of Christ dwell in you richly in all wisdom**, teaching and admonishing one another in psalms and hymns and spiritual songs, singing with grace in your hearts to the Lord." (Colossians 3: 2 – 3, 8, 12 – 15, emphasis added)

I know that was a long passage of scripture, but it is packed full of what really should be the Christian wife's anthem for how we should conduct ourselves. Scan the verse again and write down any area I have italicized you might want to work on improving. I know I need to work on all of the "put-ons" and a couple of the "put-offs" as well.

_____
_____
_____
_____
_____

Let the Law of Kindness Be in Your Mouth

The law of kindness is in the mouth of the Proverbs 31 Woman. I consider myself a kind and easy-going person; however, I have a problem with my mouth. I can say things that are in my head prior to me really thinking them entirely through. Also, because I wasn't raised by my father, I didn't have very much practice properly speaking with a man while I was growing up. I thought I would consult with the "model wife," the Proverbs 31 Woman.

> "She is a woman of strength and dignity and has no fear of old age. When she speaks, her words are wise, *and kindness is the rule for everything she says*." (Proverbs 31: 25 – 26, TLB, emphasis added)

I included the verse prior to the one about how kindness exudes from everything she speaks, because when you put the two together, it's clear she is kind, but she isn't weak. She is a strong woman, and though she respects her husband, she also respects herself.

There is abundant wisdom in the Bible that can help wives to control their tongue. The book of Proverbs says a complaining wife is like a constant dripping on a rainy day. It also says trying to stop her is like trying to hold oil in your hand. (See Proverbs 27: 15 – 16.) We don't want to be that wife, with a complaining spirit, no matter how justified we are in feeling that way.

Going Into Silent Mode

Recently, I was tempted to complain to Gordon. I wanted to have my say about someone who owed my husband some money. I was just about to send him a complaining text, when all of a sudden, my phone said, "silent mode on." Normally I have had to flip a switch on the side of my phone to activate silent mode, but I hadn't touched it. I let out this big laugh, because I knew God was telling me I needed to go into silent mode. So, I didn't text Gordon. I simply ran my bath water, connected my phone to a Bluetooth speaker, and turned on some Christian radio. I had a wonderful time, reading my Bible and listening to some uplifting music while soaking in the tub. By the time I got finished, I had a new attitude, and I wasn't worried about the person owing us money. After all, I had too many other things to do myself.

Later that evening, after Gordon ate his dinner, and we had talked and laughed about many things, I casually asked him about the person who owed him. I gave him some lighthearted advice, but I told him I knew he would handle it. And all was well.

In Conclusion

In conclusion, I want to first thank you from the bottom of my heart for purchasing and reading my book. I have lived each chapter in this book, and I know it has helped me in my marriage. I pray and believe God will do a tremendous work in your marriage too. It is my deepest desire that you would do your very best to stick to your marriage vows and give God a chance to make the day you said "I do" one of the most fulfilling and best decisions you have ever made!

May God continue to richly bless you, your husband, and the rest of your family. My prayer is for you to keep your family intact with you and your husband more in love than ever. I know God did not put this book in your hands if He did not want to bless your marriage.

Lastly, I would like for you to reflect on anything that really stuck out to you after reading this book.

Write down some next steps you are willing and able to take in the next 30 days to work on (or continue working on) your marriage.

Live with total faith in God. He is El Elyon, the Most High God. He is the Highest Sovereign of the heavens and the earth. When you praise and pray to Him, keep in mind that He's for you and he says:

> "Ask, and it will be given to you; seek, and you will find; knock, and it will be opened to you. For everyone who asks receives, and the one who seeks finds, and to the one who knocks it will be opened." (Matthew 7: 7 – 8 ESV)

Please visit my website: www.taniacscott.com, and follow me on Instagram and Facebook: @taniacscott.

Endnotes

Chapter One

    1.   21 Days to a Satisfied Life, Beth Jones, Harrison House, 67

Chapter Three

    1.   Prayers That Avail Much for Mothers, Word Ministries, Harrison House, 249

Chapter Four

    1.   His Needs, Her Needs: Building An Affair Proof Marriage, Willard F. Harley, Jr., Fleming H. Revell Company, 37
    2.   The Power of A Praying Wife, Stormie Omartian, Harvest House, 61
    3.   His Needs, Her Needs: Building An Affair Proof Marriage, Willard F. Harley, Jr., Fleming H. Revell Company, 44 – 54

Chapter Five

    1.   The Power of A Praying Wife, Stormie Omartian, Harvest House, 35

Chapter Six

    1.   "Infidelity Statistics (2022): How Much Cheating is Going On?", Paul Brian, hackspirit.com, July 4, 2022.
    2.   "Life Expectancy of Extramarital

Affairs", Sarah Ruggera, couplescounselorsandiego.com, January 17,2021.

3.   "Infidelity Statistics (2022): How Much Cheating is Going On?", Paul Brian, hackspirit.com, July 4, 2022.

4.   His Needs, Her Needs: Building An Affair Proof Marriage, William F. Farley, 27

5.   The Power of A Praying Wife, Stormie Omartian, Harvest House, 71

Chapter Seven

1.   The Power of A Praying Wife, Stormie Omartian, Harvest House, 30

2.   Supernatural Childbirth, Jackie Mize, Harrison House

3.   Prayers That Avail Much, Special Commemorative Edition, Germaine Copeland and Word Ministries, Inc., Harrison House, 190, 224, 230, 241. All of the prayers from the *"Prayers That Avail Much"* book, are online at www.prayers.org, just click the search symbol 🔍, and enter one of the prayer names I mentioned, and search other topics as well.

4.   The Power of A Praying Wife, Stormie Omartian, Harvest House, 107, 103, 49, 69, 25

Chapter Ten

1.   According to a survey of 50 married men conducted by Ruth Esumeh, 49 out of 50 chose peace over sex. Results posted by

@ruthsmarriage, on Instagram November 15, 2022.

    2.   Excerpt from the Adoration Prayer, Prayers That Avail Much, Special Commemorative Edition, Germaine Copeland and Word Ministries, Inc., Harrison House, and may be found online at www.prayers.org, just click the search symbol, and enter "Adoration Prayer ".The "Prayer of Confession" is written by Tania C. Scott.

www.ingramcontent.com/pod-product-compliance
Lightning Source LLC
Chambersburg PA
CBHW051845090426
42811CB00034B/2216/J